mississippi vegan

—

*Recipes & Stories from
a Southern Boy's Heart*

—

TIMOTHY PAKRON

AVERY

an imprint of Penguin Random House
New York

an imprint of Penguin Random House LLC
375 Hudson Street
New York, New York 10014

Most Avery books are available at special quantity discounts for bulk
purchase for sales promotions, premiums, fund-raising, and educational
needs. Special books or book excerpts also can be created to fit specific
needs. For details, write SpecialMarkets@penguinrandomhouse.com.

ISBN 9780735218147
ebook ISBN 9780735218154

Printed in China
1 3 5 7 9 10 8 6 4 2

Book and cover design by Ashley Tucker
Author's portrait by Giles Clement
All recipes, food and prop styling, and
other photography by Timothy Pakron

The recipes contained in this book are to be followed exactly as written.
The publisher is not responsible for your specific health or allergy needs
that may require medical supervision. The publisher is not responsible
for any adverse reactions to the recipes contained in this book.

—

This book is dedicated to my mama,
who is my heart.

—

contents

foreword

BY ISA CHANDRA MOSKOWITZ

What do you crave?

I'm talking deep within the belly of your soul. What makes you rush back for seconds? What makes you say, "No, I couldn't possibly . . ." but then you do?

Timmy and I met on set while shooting a cookbook of mine. I was my typical morning self, two hours late, all sloppy bun and smudged eyeliner, and he had the nerve to hug me. And kiss me! I almost spilled my coffee. I was prepared to be surly all day at anything and everything, but instead we spent the afternoon cooking and laughing, much to the annoyance of everyone around us.

At some point I saw him making mashed potatoes for no reason. "Were mashed potatoes on the shot list?" I asked, one eyebrow raised—because I can do that. He gave me his mischievous side glance. It's not a look like he did something *bad*—it's more as if he's planning a surprise birthday party for you. And those were the best mashed potatoes I've ever had.

From then on we have been inseparable. Except by a few states.

A while later, we were sitting on my couch eating roasted potatoes (I'll probably mention potatoes at least three more times in these two pages). I think of that moment all the time—because when he asked me if I wanted roasted potatoes, my immediate reaction was, "No, you dodo head. It's 1 A.M. and I have to be up at 8." And yet we sat on the couch, legs crossed, facing each other with that bowl of perfectly crispy potatoes between us, filling it back up every time it got low, and talking about everything under the sun. But mostly about potatoes.

So there's two times Timmy made me eat potatoes when I didn't think I wanted to. There were many more after that.

I think the secret to Timmy's cooking, if not Timmy himself, is cravings. Scratching that itch. Feeding those taste buds deep within the belly of your soul. But enough about Timmy. What do *you* crave?

Don't mistake this for a Southern cookbook. Well, I mean, obviously it is. It says so right in the title. And, yes, you will learn how to make a killer gumbo, but don't let it stop there because it's really a culinary footprint. In reading his stories and cooking his recipes, what I wager is that you will be inspired to follow your own cravings and explore your own history. We didn't all grow up with a garden; my yard was just a patch of cement. But Timmy's story sparks my childhood memories: snatching a meatball from my grandma's seder table. Cheese fries on the boardwalk of Coney Island. My first steamed bun from Chinatown on a brisk winter night in New York City. It awakens my cravings and inspires me to explore them. And whether you're a beginner vegan cook or the best vegan cook in the whole world like me, it will give you the tools to go forth and create your own culinary footprint.

With love from Brooklyn,
Isa Chandra

introduction

I'VE ALWAYS BEEN A SOUTHERN BOY AT HEART. I GREW UP SURROUNDED by butterflies, oak trees, and gardenias. On the Gulf Coast of Mississippi, I spent summers running barefoot through wet grass, swimming in bayous, and picking ripe blueberries warm from the sunshine. I was, and still am, profoundly impacted by my roots and the scenery of my youth. As an adult, I've kept my childlike fascination with the wild and luscious Southern landscape. I am awed and inspired by the little things: the designs of a tightly wrapped magnolia bud, the bursting hot pink color on an azalea bush, the taste of juicy loquats or the sweet nectar from a honeysuckle flower. Growing up in the midst of all of this beauty has undoubtedly had a lasting effect on me. My heart still melts at the sight of a Mississippi sunset and/ or a perfectly bloomed camellia. As a young child, I vividly remember touching the stalk of a tomato plant and thinking how magnificent the smell was. It's not very often that the actual stalk smells as intoxicating as the fruit itself, am I right? I would watch my father plant tulip bulbs and meticulously tend to his roses.

I've always known that I was more intensely connected to plants than others. At an early age, I could just tell. My eyes widened just a bit more when I spotted wildflowers, I was more excited to pick fresh strawberries, and the very thought of a citrus tree, bursting with bright clusters of fruit, resonated with me in such a way, I knew deep down that edible plants was my undeniable passion.

These days, I am even more excited because I have the chance to share this beauty with all of you. As a recipe developer and photographer, I feel as though it is my utmost responsibility to collect, create, organize, and share. As an artist, this has always been an instinct of mine, as

early as I can remember—from creating mud pie recipes to be baked on the back porch in the scorching sun, to creating an intricate nature installation in the living room (to my mother's dismay), which included a tadpole tank surrounded by a collection of rocks, crystals, bark, and leaves. My fascination with gathering small objects from nature and arranging them beautifully is still an integral part of my life today. My hands have always been busy, my eyes always curiously wondering, and my heart always craving to share.

It seems, in fact, like my entire life has prepared me for exactly this: to create a cookbook, sharing my recipes, my Southern roots, and my vegan beliefs. The recipes in this book are more than lists of ingredients and steps for preparation. Each one of them is a story: a story about the plant and mushroom kingdoms, the South, and the traditions there.

I've been a passionate vegan for over a decade now and the decision has touched every aspect of my life. The foundation of my veganism stems from my love of plants, mushrooms, animals, and the planet. I've always been incredibly sensitive and emotional, with a heightened sense of my surroundings. The mere thought of an animal being harmed, in any way, is simply *not* an option for me to support. It's not a way of eating that has ever appealed to me, either. I've always been drawn to beautiful ripe fruit, vibrant vegetables, fresh herbs, clusters of grains, nuts and seeds, peas and heirloom beans, and mushrooms. Veganism, to me, has been more of an instinct than anything. A celebration of what I do eat and how delicious it can be, while also celebrating awareness, kindness, and compassion to animals and our earth.

Now, if you had told me just a few years ago that I would be moving away from New York City and back to my native state of Mississippi to write a cookbook, I would have laughed out loud! I surprised myself with the idea of wanting to move when it first crossed my mind. What started out as a subtle tug in my heart telling me that I needed to change my surroundings soon turned into a call too loud to ignore. It just made sense. New York City is energetic, captivating, and enchanting. It was there that I created my Mississippi Vegan identity, which merged my past and my present along with all of my passions: creating recipes, taking photographs, and sharing with the world. But toward the end of the five years I lived in the bustling city, I knew in my heart it was time to leave. The city itself was like a teacher saying, "Okay, you're ready now. Go." The month before moving back, I was given the opportunity to write this very cookbook, filled with recipes and stories from my home state that celebrate plant-based cooking and reveal the beauty that remains in Mississippi. After living elsewhere for nearly twelve years, I found myself moving back to my native state to work on the most meaningful and important project of my life. Can we all say full circle?

Growing up on the Gulf Coast of Mississippi and being so close to New Orleans, I was exposed to one of the greatest culinary worlds of all time: Cajun and Creole cuisine. I was raised on some of the most delicious foods in the world. In this cookbook, I've applied everything I've learned as a passionate cook and vegan to the traditional recipes that I grew up eating, while also introducing some of the best recipes, tips, and tricks I've been exposed to during my life. I can only hope that this book will provide you with the skills to become an excellent home cook, while also showing you the love and pride that Cajun, Creole, and Southern foods are known for.

What's funny now is to look back at the time I was eating these recipes. I had no idea that I was creating a special bond with them. Of course, there's no way for you to understand the comfort that a nostalgic dish may hold when you are just a child. Simi-

lar to music, it's only after a certain amount of time that you truly understand how a particular song can touch your heart. The same concept applies to recipes. Growing up, I never thought twice about eating a scoop of mashed potatoes with gravy and what kinds of memories it might bring later in life. But now, when I take a bite of those fluffy potatoes with silky-smooth gravy, I'm propelled to that feeling of comfort I experienced as a child. These days, when I'm exposed to a new recipe that excites me, my eyes widen and my mind begins to buzz. All of the recipes in this book fall under that umbrella: a culmination of recipes that have resonated with me throughout most of my life and also some new favorites.

As a teenager, I was drawn to the world of photography, in particular the idea of *being* the photographer. The idea of organizing a composition of shapes and colors that interest me, while searching for gorgeous light, has always just made sense to me. I first started photographing my sister. Then nature. It never dawned on me to photograph food until only a few years ago. Toward the end of high school and at the beginning of college, I knew in my heart that I was an artist, through and through. Cooking has also come naturally, but I didn't always think of those two pursuits as having a connection.

During college, I compartmentalized both cooking and art. When I was in school, studying studio-art classes like sculpture, painting, and photography, I was exploring my identity and my passions while attempting to evoke emotion and beauty. Outside of class, I was constantly cooking for friends, volunteering on farms, or foraging for fruit. Cooking was my therapy—wash, cut, and organize a collection of ingredients; cook them at different stages with different herbs and spices, share them with friends and family. It still didn't click for me that cooking was art. It wasn't until I was living in New York City that I ultimately realized that the act of creating a recipe, styling the food, and photographing it to represent my passions was one of the most artistic expressions I could ever create!

The recipes and photographs in this book are much more than just pictures of food. They represent a past, a present, and a history of influences and inspiration. The act of composing instructions and ingredients for someone else to follow in order to create something beautiful and delicious is, in my opinion, magical. You could argue that it has even more impact than a piece of contemporary art. There's not only an artful image, but the instructions to help bring it to life. What's even more touching is when people cook and share a recipe with their friends, families, and loved ones. When a recipe becomes a tradition, it becomes a part of people's lives. I couldn't ask for something more touching than that.

I wrote this cookbook in a rather unconventional way. I didn't have a team of people helping me, nor did I hire a photographer or a food stylist. Instead, I had my friends help me. They graciously came from all around the world to visit me in my home in Mississippi to help me cook, document, and style the food you see on these pages. Aside from creating, the research was *constant.* Countless phone calls to my mother. "What was that one dish you always made?" or "Didn't we have that at the neighbors' Christmas party?" The majority of these recipes stem directly from my childhood, dishes that I can only remember in my mind. But others pick and pull from what I've learned throughout my life, allowing me to introduce something special and unique.

As you explore the recipes, stories, and photographs in this book, I truly hope that you are able to understand "Mississippi Vegan" as a concept. Although it may sound literal, as I am from Mississippi and I am vegan, this creative endeavor is about more than a specific location. It's a constant celebration of delicious food, memories, and pride in growing and sourcing local produce. It's an exploration of nature and a constant search for beauty that exists in this world. Coming back to my home state of Mississippi was the only place that made sense for me to write this book, and I am so happy that I did. Although I most likely will move on to other cities to explore new chapters in my life, I will always remember living here to write this book as one of the most profound experiences in my life.

As I finish writing this very introduction, my heart is heavy. It's a closing of a beautiful chapter in my life. One that I will never forget. I could never have anticipated how incredibly emotional it would be to move back to Mississippi to write this cookbook and to share it with all of you. Exploring memories, experiencing overwhelming nostalgia, and documenting the inspiration and beauty of my home state has been immensely gratifying. And although it is hard for me to let go, I know that it's now time for these stories, recipes, and photographs to touch your hearts just as much as they have touched mine.

Warmly,

Timothy

southern vegan

THERE IS AN UNDERCURRENT OF VEGANISM THAT EXISTS IN MANY food cultures, and particularly in the South. When it comes to Southern cuisine, there are many different styles and techniques of cooking with a wide array of recipes and traditions. I grew up all the way down at the bottom of Mississippi. The area I'm from is called the Gulf Coast. Seafood is abundant there, and the food is strongly influenced by our neighboring state, Louisiana, predominantly from the city of New Orleans. Southern cuisine refers generally to the traditional food from the American South, but each region is known for different ingredients and recipes. Like the ones that you will find in this book!

Now, I know what you're thinking . . . "Vegan Southern food? Yeah right!" Hear me out and I'll explain. The concept of veganism to me is a celebration of abundance: colorful vegetables, juicy sweet fruits, local and heirloom grains, a variety of nuts and seeds, and the glorious plethora of edible mushrooms. When you apply this to Southern food, it actually makes perfect sense. Let me paint the picture: okra, sweet potatoes, watermelon, black-eyed peas, collard greens, peanuts, rice, blueberries, blackberries, and pecans. There is no doubt in my mind that all of these beautiful ingredients are intrinsically Southern, in particular intrinsic to Mississippi. You ask anyone here in the 'Sip if anything on the aforementioned lists reminds them of their home state and they will agree.

The same concept applies to Cajun and Creole food. In a nutshell, Cajun food is more "country," or as I like to think, from the land. The approach is more rustic and uses an abundance of wild and native ingredients. Creole cuisine is referred to as "city food," composed of more refined dishes created in the restaurants in New Orleans. Everyone in the South, of course, has their own relationship and connection with these rich cooking traditions, which are, if you ask me, the greatest culinary achievements of the United States. What comes to my mind is buttery rice; an abundance of celery, onions, and green bell peppers; bay leaves; cayenne peppers; paprika; mirlitons; and Creole tomatoes. Now, let me ask: Are all of the ingredients I have listed in the last two paragraphs plant-based and, therefore, vegan? The answer is yes.

What Makes a Good Recipe?

That's a fantastic question. And the answer may vary from person to person. In my book (pun intended), a good recipe is accessible. A good recipe is fun to make. A good recipe should inspire you to maybe create something you've never made before or try something new with a familiar ingredient, allowing you to grow as a home cook. A good recipe is written clearly and concisely, and should make complete sense after a quick glance. A good recipe should result in excitement and pleasure. But most important, if a recipe is really good, you'll want to make it again and again and again. Which leads me to the next topic of discussion: the recipes in *this* book.

I didn't want to write a whole cookbook composed of only easy and simple recipes. Don't get me wrong, I love those kinds of recipes, the ones with only a handful of ingredients that come together quickly. But that's not really the end goal of this book. The end goal is to provide you with a collection of dishes that you most likely would not be able to easily find online. Dishes that are designed to show vegans and nonvegans alike that you can still make classic Southern dishes by only using plants and mushrooms and *not* compromise on flavor. I want this cookbook to be an invitation to push yourself just a little bit further than you normally would to make something that's incredibly delicious.

Successful Vegan Cooking

Far too often, nonvegan chefs feel as though they have succeeded in making a vegan dish just because they have removed the animal products, even if the dish is tasteless and boring. But there's much more to truly successful vegan cooking. When a chef makes a dish that is vegan, and it's also just as good as its traditional counterpart—*that's* a success. When a vegan dish is full of deep flavors and is also completely satisfying, it's not just excellent *vegan* food, it's excellent *food*. Period.

Coaxing those deep flavors is the key. Many traditional recipes call for what I refer to as a "singular sum" ingredient. An example of this is andouille sausage in gumbo. Now, on the ingredient list you'll just see, "1 pound andouille sausage." But in reality, andouille is not only pork, it's cayenne pepper, paprika, onion, garlic, spices, and herbs; not to mention it's smoked, which adds a whole other dimension of flavor. It's one ingredient that actually contains a multitude of ingredients. The point I'm trying to make is that it's no wonder people feel as though certain vegan recipes, especially compared to their traditional nonvegan recipes, are lackluster or missing something: They are. They're missing a lot!

When I cook, I'm always thinking about how to bring in that rich taste. Sometimes it's adding more herbs and spices or combining unlikely ingredients. I also love to use ingredients that are more concentrated in flavor (more on that in a minute). In other recipes, one or two *key* plant-based ingredients creates a distinct flavor profile. For example, we associate fennel seeds and sage with a meaty, sausage flavor. Our brain is trained to recognize those two ingredients together as "sausage." Add these herbs to any kind of dense, hearty texture and you can create something that tastes like sausage.

Sometimes it's a combination of textures that makes a dish. Take, for example, a fried shrimp po' boy and its combination of toasted flaky bread, shredded lettuce, juicy tomatoes, a healthy amount of mayo, and a protein that is battered and deep-fried. All of those elements working together is what *really* makes the recipe. It's not *all* about the shrimp.

I'm always trying techniques to up the "oomph" factor and elevate vegan cooking to something truly delicious. Now let's address some of the other concepts to understand successful vegan cooking. First up, umami.

Umami

Umami means savory, or more specifically, a "pleasant savory taste." Umami is one of the five basic tastes, along with sour, sweet, bitter, and salty. Some common examples of umami-rich ingredients are pork, dried fish, and cheese. But guess what? Some other common examples—in fact, the *best* examples in my humble opinion—are completely vegan. Ayyyy! Soy sauce or tamari, miso, shiitake and morel mushrooms, dried seaweed, and nutritional yeast are all very concentrated with umami. What this means is they have high concentrations of naturally occurring glutamate, or glutamic acid, an amino acid that provides a savory and delicious flavor to food. There are also certain vegetables that have umami, such as corn, potatoes, asparagus, and, the most notorious for containing umami, ripe tomatoes. To understand umami, imagine a super ripe, juicy, cherry tomato bursting in your mouth. When your tongue enjoys the fantastic flavor of richness, causing it to salivate and crave more. *That's* umami.

I'll admit it's tough to compete with animal products that are rich in umami such as bacon, seafood, and parmesan cheese. But I've got some tricks up my sleeve, and by combining multiple umami-laden ingredients, I can get pretty close. You may be surprised to see a tablespoon of tamari or miso, a scoop of tomato paste, dried shiitakes, or a sprinkling of nutritional yeast in some of these recipes. But these hero ingredients are plant- and mushroom-based powerhouses. They take my vegan cooking to the next level.

Aged Ingredients

Another secret weapon for successful vegan cooking is using aged ingredients. Just like parmesan cheese ripens and cured meats concentrate in flavor, there are many examples of aged, vegan-friendly items that pack an umami punch or complex flavor. Some of these ingredients are ones we met in the last section: tamari or soy sauce and miso. Other examples include kimchi, sauerkraut, nut cheeses fermented with probiotics, wine, vinegar, olives, sourdough breads, and kombucha.

There's no doubt that fresh produce and whole foods are an integral part of a vegan foodie's kitchen, but fermented and aged products are just as important. What I have found is that balancing these ingredients is what makes for a beautiful recipe. It's the contrast that makes for a harmonious relationship, and the results are undeniably delicious.

Dried Ingredients

The last thing that I would like to address in the flavor department is dried ingredients. When all of the moisture is removed from a piece of fresh fruit, vegetable, or mushroom, the flavor is concentrated. I love to cook with ingredients such as sundried tomatoes, dehydrated mushrooms and fruit, and powders such as onion and garlic for that extra depth of flavor.

The Mississippi Vegan Pantry

In this section, you'll find more information about all of the ingredients that I personally love and feel obligated to highlight. There are also a few ingredients that might make you do a double take when you're scanning through a recipe. Sometimes I do call for a few special ingredients that you may have to order off the Internet or find at a specialty store. But don't worry, I've provided a page on my website (mississippivegan.com) where you can find all of the ingredients that I refer to and personally recommend (and use). That said, I strive to make my recipes accessible and approachable, with ingredients that you can mostly source year-round and at your local grocery store. If I do call for an ingredient that may be hard to find, I will most likely provide a more accessible substitution. That said, don't let not having one ingredient stop you from making one of my recipes. That's silly. I just want to give you some inspiration to hop into the kitchen and make something delicious, even if it's not the *exact* same recipe.

Throughout the recipes in this book, you may notice some unique herbs that you might not be familiar with. These are ones that I personally grow after years and years of research and spending way too much time at the farmers' market. I totally understand that you might not have lime basil or lemon thyme, but the goal of including these varieties is to inspire you to grow them yourself or to look for them at your local farmers' market. You'd be surprised what you can find if you really look. I was, myself, when I moved back to Mississippi. When I first visited my local market here in Jackson, I found garlic chives, blue spice basil, purple Napa cabbage, cheese pumpkin, white turmeric, and green meat radishes! Here in Mississlippery! The point is, go to your local farmers' market as often as you can and look for unique herbs and produce. You will not only be supporting local farmers, but you'll be providing yourself with healthier ingredients, which will in return make you healthier. Not to mention, the fresher the produce, the better your food tastes.

Store-Bought Vegan Products

A common misconception about veganism is that because we choose to not consume animal-based products, we have to reinvent the wheel or make everything from scratch. There's an expectation that we won't or shouldn't use packaged products. Here's my opinion: Everyone needs to chill. While I like to use fresh and homemade ingredients whenever I can, I don't mind using some store-bought ingredients. It's easy for day-to-day cooking, and there honestly has never been a more exciting time on the market for new plant-based products. Currently, there is a wide range of artisanal, high-quality products across the board, from smoked vegan meats and aged nut cheeses to creamy coconut yogurts. The "processed" products are becoming less and less processed, and the ingredients are becoming better and better. Personally, I am happy and excited to support vegan companies and also nonvegan companies with vegan options. Supporting these companies and products lets them know that there is a market, effectively spreading vegan awareness and supporting sustainability overall. It's undeniable that *everyone* should be questioning their consumption habits and support the idea of moving in a more positive direction. Supporting vegan companies is a great way to start. You can find some of my favorite brands on my website: mississippivegan.com/shop.

VEGAN MEATS In this book, there are many vegan renditions of meats using a variety of different ingredients. Some use mushrooms like shiitakes (Shiitake Bacon, page 254) as the base or a combination of plant-based ingredients such as wheat gluten and barley (Barley Sausage, page 57). What truly makes the meat delicious is all of the seasoning and spices, and the cooking techniques you use. The goal is to re-create the *experience* of meat, not to convince you that shiitake mushrooms and pork are the same exact thing. They're not! And that's totally okay. When the final product tastes just as good as the original, it simply shouldn't matter. And if an animal's life can be saved in order to enjoy the very textures and flavors we all love, that's a win in my book.

VEGAN CHEESES Dairy-based cheese is a delicious, flavorful, and incredibly satisfying ingredient that chefs and home cooks alike rely on heavily. Why on earth would vegans *not* want to re-create this magical ingredient in our recipes? In this book, there are a handful of recipes that create cheesy-tasting components by using ingredients such as miso, nutritional yeast, and nuts. In other more traditional Southern recipes, I call for store-bought vegan cheese. I do so because that's what makes the original recipes so easy and delicious. If a traditional recipe called for an aged block of parmesan, most people would buy it at the store rather than try to make it themselves. The same is true for vegans! Don't get me wrong—I love making homemade staples, and I've even included some of those recipes in this book. It can be a lot of fun. But requiring a home cook to make every element in a recipe from scratch is asking *a lot*. My biggest goal is to help make these recipes become new, everyday classics in your home.

VEGAN BUTTER is delicious and convenient, and a fantastic ingredient to use in any dish for the *same exact reasons* home cooks and chefs use traditional dairy butter. Just like in the nonvegan food world, there are both processed margarines as well as incredible, high-end artisanal vegan butters.

VEGAN MAYO has become more accessible and more popular than ever! And rightfully so, it *is* delicious. There are a variety of different brands available on the market, some made from organic vegetable oils and others from chickpea water (also known as aquafaba). You can now find vegan mayo next to traditional mayo or in the refrigerated section of natural food stores. If you are keen on making your own vegan mayo, you can find my foolproof recipe on page 262.

NUTRITIONAL YEAST is probably my most favorite ingredient in the world. Seriously. It's an inactive yeast that grows on beet molasses or sugar cane. Once it's processed and packaged, you are left with a tan, flaky powder that is bursting with a savory flavor. But why? Well, because it has a high concentration of the previously mentioned glutamic acid, which makes foods taste delicious. If I had to pinpoint it exactly, I would say it tastes like a chicken bouillon cube with an overall nuttiness and cheesiness. As you can imagine, this flavor is quite hard to find in the plant- and mushroom-based world, so I find this ingredient to be invaluable. There are many different forms of nutritional yeast on the market, some are powdered and some are flakes. I prefer the flakes. You can find "nooch" in small jars at the store, but I buy mine only in the bulk section. To store, I recommend keeping the flakes in a tightly sealed jar in the fridge. This keeps the nutritional yeast dry, crisp, and away from light. One trick I've learned (you will see it throughout the book) is that toasting the flakes enhances their flavor.

UME PLUM VINEGAR is pickling brine from umeboshi plums, sea salt, and red shiso. This crimson-colored vinegar is very salty, so please be cautious when using any amount. Its unique tartness can make a dull recipe burst with robust flavor.

RICE VINEGAR, with a mild, delicate flavor, is less harsh than traditional white vinegar. It's my go-to when cooking. Whether using it with vegetables, in rice, or in a salad dressing, rice vinegar can perk up any recipe.

BAY LEAVES are one of my absolute favorite ways to season rice, potatoes, soups, and stews. You can use fresh or dried leaves. I adore their fresh flavor, as it is more robust and grassy. If you're having a hard time pinpointing exactly what these beautiful leaves taste like, try making the Bay Leaf Tea (page 275). It's the best way to experience their delightfully peppery and grassy flavor. You can usually find fresh bay leaves in the refrigerated section at most grocery stores, next to the other packaged herbs or in the dried herb section. My father has a tree in his backyard, so that's how I stock up!

KOMBU is an edible kelp (a type of seaweed) that has a high concentration of glutamic acid, making recipes taste delicious. You can purchase this sea vegetable dried, in sheets, and use small amounts to help season broths or beans, similar to a bay leaf. This sea vegetable is also known for helping to break down the carbohydrates in beans, making them easier to digest.

CAYENNE PEPPER is a powder made from dried and ground chili peppers; it has become a staple seasoning in Southern, Cajun, and Creole cuisine. I find the spice it provides to dishes addicting and I'm always reaching for it! Even if you only use a little, the tickle it provides the tongue is truly unique and can quickly elevate a recipe from boring to exciting.

MUSHROOMS hold a very special place in my heart. I absolutely adore them. And I truly believe that they are the "meat" of a healthy vegan diet. The mushroom kingdom is so incredibly fascinating, and I am learning more and more about it each day. Not only are there delicious, edible mushrooms, there are also medicinal ones that are highly beneficial for a variety of different reasons. (For the most part, I'm going to stick to the culinary ones in this book, but I do have a medicinal recipe on page 273.) You will notice that some of the mushrooms I cook with are wild. This means they grow in nature, undisturbed by humans. Foraging mushrooms is

no joke, people; it's very serious business. I'm certainly not recommending you go searching for mushrooms and pop them willy-nilly into your mouth. No! But what I do hope to do is inspire you to educate yourself and to learn more about the process. Of course, if the idea of foraging mushrooms scares you, then leave that to the local foragers, farmers, and restaurants. But if you are interested in foraging for mushrooms, or are interested in learning more about the medicinal ones, you can hop on over to mississippivegan.com/shop to see what books I recommend. Here are a few wild and cultivated mushrooms that I personally love:

Shiitakes are a personal favorite because they are the most widely accessible, flavorful mushroom on the market, rich in umami, fragrant in smell, and chewy in texture. Do note that there are standard, thin shiitakes that look like pancakes and a thicker, more meaty variety that have stretch marks, sometimes referred to as "Chinese shiitakes." You can find these at most Asian markets. I actually prefer them over the traditional variety, as I find them to be more robust and flavorful. Check out my Shiitake Bacon recipe on page 254 to see them pictured.

Chanterelle mushrooms are very special to me because they grow wild and in abundance here in Mississippi! Lucky for me, the first year I moved back down here was a prolific year. I'm talking buckets and buckets of chanterelles. They have a delicately fibrous texture, similar to chicken, and a buttery, nutty flavor. If you harvest them fresh, sometimes their smell is reminiscent of apricots. I have seen them pop up at supermarkets more and more, so keep an eye out!

Lion's Mane is a fascinating mushroom that is stark white and grows in a structure similar to a lion's mane! This mushroom grows wild throughout North America, and I've had the pleasure of finding some here in Mississippi. Best known for its texture, this mushroom is reminiscent of crabmeat. This mushroom can also be cultivated indoors, so I predict that it will become more widely accessible in years to come. Note that I have seen this variety pop up at farmers' markets in larger cities, so keep that in mnd while shopping.

Dried Morels are fantastic because they provide the chance to try what is known to be one of the most highly sought after mushrooms in the world. Morels grow only in the wild, are very difficult to find, and have a very short window of time when

mushroom tips

—

When storing fresh mushrooms, keep them in a paper bag that is tightly folded closed on top so they will last longer. If they dry out a little bit, that's okay. You want to avoid storing mushrooms in plastic bags so they don't become slimy. If this happens, toss them.

When cleaning mushrooms, some people say to never rinse them. I think that's silly. I've seen the way people handle bulk mushrooms at the grocery store and I'm not about to just gently brush them off before eating them. No ma'am, thank you, Pam! I will most definitely be washing my store-bought mushrooms. The best way to do so is to rinse the mushrooms under running water until you feel they are sufficiently washed. Drain the mushrooms thoroughly and transfer them to a large salad spinner. Spin, spin, spin, and voilà! You are left with clean and dry mushrooms, ready to go. I've never noticed a difference in flavor by cleaning them this way and I doubt you will either. Now, when it comes to **wild mushrooms** that you forage, bring a small brush and quickly wipe off any dirt after you've picked them, cleaning them as you go. If the mushrooms have multiple crevices, such as morels or lion's mane, you will have to clean them to remove any grit and check them for critters. If they are covered in dirt, simply use the salad spinner method mentioned above, while using a damp paper towel to help remove any dirt if need be. Do note that any wild mushroom should be thoroughly cooked before consumed.

Dried mushrooms, in particular wild dried mushrooms, may have some grit as well. As you can guess, even the smallest amount of grit can completely ruin an entire recipe. Therefore, I always recommend soaking dried mushrooms. Then I rinse the rehydrated mushrooms thoroughly to remove any grit and use them as the recipe calls for. You can strain the soaking liquid through a coffee filter or fine-mesh sieve. This will eliminate any debris, leaving you with amazing mushroom broth, ready to go. Try this technique in my Mushroom Rigatoni Casserole (page 185).

they grow in the spring. I've found wild morels *once* thus far in my life, and let me tell you, it was one of the most exciting feelings in the world. I quickly brought them inside, pan-fried them with a little oil, sprinkled them with salt, and devoured them. They are one of the richest, meatiest, and most flavorful mushrooms that I've ever had the pleasure of eating. Although incredibly expensive, I personally think morels are worth every penny.

KALA NAMAK is a salt that has naturally occurring sulfur. It is usually ground into a very fine powder and provides the perfect "eggy" flavor for vegan recipes replicating eggs. Whether you sprinkle it on top of a soup, salad, or sandwich, this salt provides an impressive pop of flavor.

MALDON SALT is simply sea salt that has gone through a special process that results in a flaky, crispy, crunchy texture. It truly elevates a dish to amazing. I love sprinkling this stuff on top of cookies, salads, or pasta dishes. Smoked Maldon salt is also available.

SMOKED SEA SALT is an amazing vegan secret weapon. Providing an intense depth of flavor to soups, stews, and sauces, this ingredient is instrumental in making a vegan recipe taste authentic to its nonvegan counterpart.

SEA SALT is my preferred choice of everyday salt, and that's what I use predominantly throughout this book. When used, I will always give my suggested measurement. For example: "1 teaspoon sea salt, or to taste." This means if you are sensitive to salt, please start with a smaller amount than suggested and add more if desired. That means I don't want to hear any complaints about a recipe being too salty, folks! I can't physically be in your kitchen to season every recipe to your liking, now can I?

TRUFFLE SALT is usually sea salt that has been infused with particles of dried truffles. It is an incredibly cost-effective way to get that gorgeous truffle flavor without breaking the bank. Do note that a little goes a long way, and a small jar can last you for up to a year. I recommend using this as a finishing salt, as the flavor is delicate and can easily be lost if used too early in a recipe.

TRUFFLE OIL is much like the aforementioned truffle salt in that it has been infused with truffles. If you're not familiar, a truffle is an exquisitely flavorful mushroom that grows underground. Because truffles are wild and rare, they are extremely expensive and difficult to source. Infused oil is a fantastic way to preserve their flavor while also having a long shelf life. A drizzle of this stuff over pasta, soup, or popcorn is a game changer. Do note that white truffles are more fragrant and aromatic compared with black truffles. This explains why white truffle oil and salt are more expensive—and totally worth it if you ask me. You can find out what brands of salt and oil I personally use on my website: mississippivegan.com/shop.

TAMARI or gluten-free soy sauce is one of my most often used and favorite condiments. Rich, salty, and, dare I say, buttery, tamari is absolutely loaded with a savoriness that one can only refer to as umami. You will find I use it in almost all of my savory recipes because, well, it's fantastic. If you're soy-free, don't fret! Coconut aminos is a similar product that doesn't have quite the depth of flavor as tamari, but it's close and can easily be used as a replacement.

MISO PASTE can be made from a variety of different grains or beans that are mashed into a paste and combined with koji spores. After this ferments for months, you are left with an intricately flavorful condiment. Tangy, cheesy, salty, and sometimes sweet, this umami-rich ingredient is incredibly important in many of these recipes. If you are not familiar with this ingredient, I urge you to find some immediately. Look in the refrigerated section of your grocery store, by the tofu or tempeh, as this is a raw product, rich in probiotics. For this reason, I personally avoid purchasing the pasteurized variety. The most commonly found miso is made from fermented soybeans, but if you are soy-free, chickpea miso has become increasingly more available. I find it to be a equally as subtle as mellow white miso, which is what I use in most of my recipes.

GARLIC POWDER is garlic cloves that are dried and then ground into a fine powder. Now, don't be fooled! There are "garlic powders" out there that are granules and are not a powder. But the bottle still reads "powder." Infuriating, I

say! But, you can use your noodle and quite simply see that even though the title on the bottle might say powder, it is in fact not. I recommend using the powder form, as it is more effective in coating ingredients and dissolving into recipes. Garlic powder has a deep, rich flavor that's slightly sweet. It's very different from raw garlic or cooked garlic, so don't think you can skip this ingredient.

ONION POWDER is dried onion ground into a fine powder. This powder, just like garlic powder, is intensely rich in flavor, with a slight sweetness. It is different from raw or cooked onion—think veggie broth powderesque. Both onion powder and garlic powder provide a beautifully rich depth of flavor for soups, stews, casseroles, dips, etc. I will often combine the powders with their raw and cooked counterpart so that I'm adding 2x to 3x of the ingredient. (See more on 2x to 3x on page 41.)

LIQUID SMOKE is one of those magical ingredients that's cheap, incredibly potent, and helps to create that meaty flavor, without the meat. Replicating the effect of what would normally take hours for a smoker to do, just add a few drops of this stuff and you're good to go. Do note that brands vary in strength and bitterness. For consistency's sake, I personally recommend using Colgin brand liquid smoke for my recipes, as it's delicious and not too bitter. If using other brands, I always recommend using less and adding more if you need to. Using too much can ruin a recipe.

TOASTED SESAME OIL provides a rich, nutty flavor that adds a beautiful complexity to dishes. Drizzled on rice, hummus, or vegetables sides, this oil can truly highlight a dish. A splash or two in a sauce can also provide an underlying butteriness. I use this oil frequently in my kitchen and recipes. Do note that a little goes a long way.

MEYER LEMONS are one of my favorite ingredients because of their earthy, sweet flavor—it's much bolder than regular lemon juice. The zest is also a fantastic source of flavor. Of course, you can always use regular lemons if you can't find this variety. But if you ever see Meyer lemons at your local store, do yourself a favor and grab some.

GINGER is a bright yellow root with a tan, papery skin. I always have some in my fridge. It has powerful anti-inflammatory properties and is also known for helping an upset stomach. I personally love the heat that it provides, which is different from a traditional spicy component. I predominantly use fresh ginger. It's perfect for hot teas, beverages, soups, and salad dressings. I find dried, powdered ginger to be quite different in flavor and best for baking. When peeling ginger, use a spoon to scrape off the skin. Because the root is very fibrous, I recommend either roughly chopping before blending and using a Microplane or mincing finely with a knife if placing directly in a recipe.

TURMERIC is similar to ginger, as they both are pungent, knobby roots. And yes, they are related. Turmeric has a papery skin with a flesh ranging in color from yellow to white to, most common, bright orange. I use fresh turmeric in soup, teas, and juice for its variety of medicinal properties. I use dried turmeric powder mainly for its color. It is an ideal way to impart a beautiful yellow or orange hue to a dish, depending on how much you use and what other spices you combine it with.

VEGETABLE BROTH is a fantastic ingredient that can elevate the flavor of a recipe, whether it be soups and stews, rice and pasta, or sauces and gravy. You can easily purchase vegetable broth at the store or you can make your own by saving your vegetable scraps. I also recommend investing in some vegetable broth powder or bouillon paste/cubes. They are loaded with flavor. Simply add water and mix to make your own broth.

MUSHROOM BROTH is my *favorite* broth to use because you can make it easily and quickly on the spot, at home. Dried shiitake mushrooms and boiling water create a beautifully rich, buttery, savory broth. In vegan cooking, this broth is a game changer. It has an elevated flavor profile compared to just vegetable broth, one that has much more of a leg to stand on when being compared to chicken or beef stock.

WORCESTERSHIRE SAUCE is a condiment and traditional ingredient used in Southern, Cajun, and Creole cuisine. Made with soy sauce, tamarind paste, and oftentimes, dried fish, this umami-rich condiment provides a salty, tangy bite to recipes. There are multiple vegan and gluten-free Worcestershire sauces available on the market today, in stores and online. I buy mine in bulk as it's easy to store and you can never have too much.

PLANT-BASED MILKS have flooded the market, with stores boasting dozens of brands that fill up nearly half the diary aisle in the supermarket. That said, I've never been a huge fan of store-bought plant-based milk as I find that it can taste a bit stale. If I'm cooking or baking, I will use plain unsweetened soy milk, as I find the flavor to be the most neutral while also providing a milky texture. My favorite variety is the kind in the nondairy milk section that is not refrigerated. The ingredients should say: water and soybeans. That's it. I despise all the weird additives and preservatives.

CASHEW CREAM/MILK is simply raw cashews blended up with water. Depending on the ratio, you are left with a thick creamy texture or a more liquidy milky texture. It's entirely up to you and the recipe you need it for. The reason I am so drawn to this form of cream/milk is because I can make as much as I need on the spot and it's absolutely delicious. No stale taste, no preservatives or additives or—my pet peeve—vanilla flavoring. With regard to soaking, this can be a bit controversial, but I personally *do not* soak my cashews. The reason for this is because I have a high-powered blender and I have never had any issues when it comes to blending. I simply throw in raw cashews and my desired amount of water and I always have the smoothest, creamiest results, no soaking required. Depending on your blender, you can simply soak the cashews in boiling water for 15 minutes to soften them if need be.

VANILLA SUGAR is simply granulated sugar that has been infused with vanilla bean pods. Simply add your desired sugar (preferably organic and unbleached) to a jar and throw in one or two vanilla bean pods. You'll be amazed when you open a jar after only a few days to find the sugar bursting with vanilla flavor. In my kitchen, I keep a small jar of granulated sugar for savory recipes and one very large jar of vanilla sugar for my desserts and sweets.

COCONUT CREAM is heaven on earth. Traditionally, heavy cream is whipped up into a delightful, fluffy texture with added sugar for sweetness. The same concept applies to coconut cream. Because this plant-based cream is high in fat, it will solidify when it's cold. All you have to do is place the can of full-fat coconut milk in the refrigerator for a couple of hours. Once chilled, turn it upside down, open it up, and once the liquid is poured out, you are left with rich, creamy, and decadent coconut cream. The texture is divine—creamy, smooth, soft, and buttery. With a little vanilla, sugar, and a beating with a hand mixer, you can make outstanding whipped cream. Once frozen, it will transform into ice cream! Check out the Peach Cream Pops (page 240) or the Strawberry Shortcake Crunch Bars (page 233) to see this stuff in action. Do note that sometimes, but not often, you'll buy a can of coconut milk that may be a "dud." This means the fat will not solidify into cream when it is refrigerated. You can save this can for sauces, soups, or curries. I always recommend buying an extra can or two when using coconut cream in a recipe. I've also seen pure coconut cream sold in the same section where you find coconut milk.

SORGHUM SYRUP OR SORGHUM MOLASSES is a traditional Southern ingredient that I have become accustomed to using in my cooking, especially sweets. It's similar to blackstrap molasses in that it's a thick and sweet syrup, but instead of being derived from sugar cane, it comes from the sorghum plant. I find it to be much milder than traditional molasses, being less bitter and lighter in color. I love using it in recipes, because it not only provides a sweetness, but a rich flavor with notes of caramel, vanilla, and coffee.

COCONUT SUGAR has been popping up everywhere these days. And rightfully so! It's a delicious alternative to plain, white granulated sugar. Not only does it have a toasty, caramelly flavor, but it has vitamins and minerals as well. A great example of how to use this sugar is in Mama's Pralines (page 243).

BROWN RICE SYRUP has been around for a long time, but I just recently started to use it. It has the texture of honey and a mild caramel flavor. You can easily substitute it in recipes that call for honey or use it in recipes where you need a chewiness.

Kitchen Equipment (You Might Not Have)

I'm very proud of my collection of kitchen tools. And you should be proud of yours, too! Shopping for kitchen gadgets that will allow me to perform more effectively in the kitchen is not only fun but satisfying. Now, I could sit here all day and talk about this topic, but, to be honest, I really don't think you need me to tell you to invest in a sharp knife, pot, or muffin pan, eh? Instead I'm just going to mention some of the tools you might not be as familiar with that I personally love and use every day.

HANDHELD JULIENNE PEELER is one of my favorite kitchen tools. It's an incredibly simple and safer (compared to a mandoline) way to make beautiful julienned strips of vegetables. This tool looks like a regular vegetable peeler, but the blade is shaped to cut matchstick-style strips. Of course, you can simply use a sharp knife, but I find that the handheld julienne peeler is more efficient. Whether it's carrots, cucumbers, squash, or zucchini, fresh strips of julienned vegetables are a lovely addition to salads and soups, or can be used as a garnish. I honestly use mine every day!

MANDOLINES are incredibly dangerous. The only reason I suggest having one is for those times when you want to slice things *paper* thin effortlessly. Some examples in the book are thinly sliced red onions for a sandwich, or thinly sliced apples to make "apple roses" (page 236). That said, please be incredibly careful when using one by wearing gloves, using the guard that's included in the kit, or using only half of the ingredient you're slicing. You can always find a use for that leftover piece of apple, carrot, or zucchini. Heck, just feed it to the dog if you must! But don't think just because you are using a mandoline that you have to go all the way to the tip of the vegetable—yikes! Don't be silly.

CUTTING BOARDS are obviously a no-brainer, but here's my two cents. I recommend a large, thick wooden one with grips on the bottom for everyday use. This prevents the board from moving around and the thickness prevents warping. Use it for savory ingredients such as vegetables, onions, and garlic. Next, I recommend storing a second, smaller cutting board and using it only for fruits and sweets. I can't tell you how frustrating it is to take a bite out of a watermelon or a piece of banana bread that tastes like onions. If your board doesn't have grips, simply place a damp paper towel underneath it to prevent moving.

RICE COOKERS Obviously, you can make rice in a pot. But you have to watch it and you can easily mess it up. With rice cookers, you simply set it and forget it. Once the rice is done, it turns off. Not to mention, it comes out perfectly every time. I use mine constantly and I love it. If you do invest in one, you will notice that the bottom of the rice may "burn" or become crispy. This is considered a delicacy by many, including me. It's toasty, crunchy, and delicious. After the rice has cooled completely, I've noticed it is easier to scrape up from the bottom.

CAST IRON Cast-iron cookware is my favorite. First, it's indestructible. Second, once heated thoroughly, it provides even cooking for not only sautéing but baking as well. Third, after cast iron is seasoned, it becomes naturally nonstick. I have cast-iron pots, skillets of all sizes, loaf and cornbread pans, and casserole dishes to boot. They're also very easy to maintain. Here are my tips: To clean, use a brush or sponge with *no soap*, only water shortly after using. You can use coarse sea salt to help remove the nitty-gritty if need be. Next, completely dry with a towel. Spray or drizzle vegetable oil on the cast iron and massage it all over. That's it!

FINE-MESH SIEVES are ideal for straining any blended-up ingredient with pulp you would like to remove or draining any kind of bean, pea, or grain. I have a variety of sizes and literally use them every day.

SMALL BLENDERS OR MINI-FOOD PROCESSORS are perfect if you don't want to have some big to-do when you're making a simple recipe. They are ideal for sauces, condiments, or anything you need blended up in small amounts.

CHEESECLOTH is a fine-mesh cloth that can be used to make cheeses, nut milks, vegetable juices, and more. The best part? It's reusable. I simply rinse mine well after each use and hang it to dry. It's dyed bright orange from all the raw turmeric root I juice, and I'm totally okay with that.

Tips Worth Mentioning

SHARPEN YOUR KNIVES. I highly recommend sharpening your knives often—at least once a week—at home using a honing rod. Do your research and figure out which one would be best for you and how to use it. You can also have your knives sharpened professionally, which I do once every few months in combination with my honing rod. Ask your local kitchen supply store or favorite small local restaurant for a recommendation. This ensures that your knives are sharp as hell and ready to go.

USE STORE-BOUGHT INGREDIENTS! Don't get it twisted—I love making things from scratch. Honestly, most of the recipes in this book *are* made from scratch, with few or no products. That said, don't make things more difficult when they don't need to be. If you are in a pinch or don't have time, feel free to substitute whatever will make your life easier and the recipe more accessible. I personally love to take advantage of frozen pie crust and puff pastry, both of which are available in vegan options.

ALWAYS USE FRESHLY CRACKED BLACK PEPPER. Do yourself a favor and invest in a peppermill. I'm talking a cool peppermill. One that stands proud on the kitchen counter. One that is built well and sturdy. This not only makes grinding pepper fun and easy, but it ensures that you are getting the most flavorful and fresh pepper for your recipes. If you hop around all of the recipes in this book, you'll notice that I always say "freshly cracked pepper." And I'm serious. I do not use preground pepper just like I don't use preground coffee. I want it to be as fresh as possible. Lucky for you and me, whole peppercorns are easy to source and are even easier to freshly grind on food.

BUY BULK PRODUCE THAT KEEPS. I always have an abundance of potatoes, onions, garlic, and shallots, which I keep on the counter; and lemons, limes, celery, carrots, and fresh ginger, which I keep in the fridge. This is for two reasons. 1) I use these ingredients every day. 2) They have a long shelf life and are easy to store. If your celery stalks begin to look limp, simply cut off the ends and place in a jar of water. They will plump back up in no time.

DON'T STORE TOMATOES IN THE FRIDGE. This always infuriates me, as it will make them mealy. Please leave them on the counter. Tomatoes should be purchased frequently, in small amounts, and consumed quickly.

DON'T BUY DRIED HERBS IN BULK. Buying in bulk is not usually the answer, unless you are cooking for a very large family or you work at a cafe or restaurant. The reason for this is because you want to make sure that even if the herbs or spices are dried, they are still fresh. I remember making some soup when visiting my parents one weekend. I tasted it, turned my head, looked at my mother, and said, "It tastes stale." We then quickly looked at all of her oils, herbs, and spices. Let me tell you—she was mortified. The oil was expired, the garlic powder was from 1986 (when I was born), the dried thyme was in a shaker that looked like it was designed from the '70s, and the black pepper was musky. During my next visit, I was pleased to find that she had updated the spices, oils, and herbs in her cabinet with freshly stocked replacements. Let this be a lesson to all of you. Buy small amounts, use them quickly, and replace them often.

STORE FRESH HERBS WELL. Fresh herbs can be stored in a tightly sealed bag and container with a damp paper towel for quite a long time in the fridge. Using this method, I've been pleasantly surprised to find a bunch of thyme or oregano in perfect shape that was more than two weeks old. If it smells bad or there is mold, obviously do not consume.

Recipe Notes

A DASH OR PINCH MEANS LESS THAN ⅛ TEASPOON. As you can imagine, this would be annoying to measure and silly to make a spoon for. Use your fingers, add a pinch, and stop making things so complicated.

2X TO 3X INGREDIENTS is a concept first introduced to me by the Cajun/Creole chef Paul Prudhomme. The basic idea is an ingredient in multiple forms that are used at different stages in a recipe. Let's say onions in a soup. First, you have the onions that are sautéed in the beginning of the recipe. By the end, they are sweet, caramelized, and basically mush. If you add onion powder to the seasoning/spice blend, that's 2x. When you add raw onion toward the end of the recipe, you're providing that fresh spice onion offers while also a crunchier texture. That's 3x onion. Get my drift?

LOVE YOUR WHISK. Use a whisk to rapidly blend all your dry ingredients together when you're baking. This will get rid of any clumps and eliminate the need to use a sifter. If you do not already own a whisk, go buy one because that's just ridiculous.

ZEST BEFORE JUICING. When zesting any citrus, make sure to do so before juicing! I can't tell you how frustrating it can be to juice a lemon or lime and then realize that you need zest as well. A good recipe should call for the zest before the juice, but if that's not the case, you could be in for a problem. When zesting, avoid the spongy white part of the peel, as it is bitter. Only use the brightly colored zest layer.

SCAN THE RECIPES FIRST! This is a great way to prevent running into any problems during your recipe making. To prepare for your shopping trip, always thoroughly scan the ingredient list and then make a list of things that you will need. Check your pantry or fridge for things you may have already. I also recommend scanning the recipe to prepare yourself for what's ahead. Is there soaking time? Does the dough need to rise? Does something need to chill? Does something need to set? Overnight, in the fridge? Don't throw your hands up in a tantrum because you have to let the dough rise for an hour. If you had scanned the recipe, you wouldn't be upset and cursing me!

BE PROUD OF YOUR KITCHEN. I'm serious as a heart attack, people! Take pride in your kitchen. Keep it clean, keep it organized. A happy kitchen makes for a happy cook. And a happy cook makes the best-tasting food. It's a proven fact! I highly recommend having a designated spot for everything. I keep all of my bulk foods in beautiful glass jars, tightly sealed. My spices are easy to see and grab. I have a collection of oils, vinegars, and most often used spices in a beautiful arrangement on my counter, next to the stove. I always have fresh flowers and nice candles to enrich the space. I use environmentally friendly cleaning products that smell amazing so that I look forward to wiping down the counters. I sweep almost every day and mop once a week to keep the floors nice and clean. I make sure to keep the cupboards organized and uncluttered. When I walk into the kitchen, I love seeing it clean and organized. This makes me proud and excited to cook. The best part is when people come over and say, "Wow! Your kitchen is amazing."

Finally, **lagniappe** is a word used in New Orleans and along the Gulf Coast that means "a little something extra" or "added bonus." Traditionally, cookbooks will have tips provided with each recipe. Throughout the recipes in this book, I will refer to them as "Lagniappe." Why? Because it's cute.

Mississippivegan.com/shop

If you need help in the shopping department, I've got you covered. On my website, I have a page dedicated to all of my favorite ingredients, kitchen tools, and particular books that I love. Of course, these are only products that I personally use and recommend. For the most part, I try not to call for for specific brands in this book as the market is constantly changing, especially when it comes to vegan cheeses, butters, and milks. The page on my website will be the best resource to see what I recommend to use for the best results in my recipes.

Mississippivegan.com/playlists

Music is equally as important to me as food. Creating and cooking go hand in hand for me. Because I find music so incredibly important, I have dedicated a page on my website to my personal playlists. Each playlist is customized for a variety of different occasions, in particular while cooking or for dinner parties. Enjoy!

CHAPTER 1

—

breakfast,
breads
&
biscuits

toasted pecan waffles

with bananas Foster topping

MAKES 8 TO 12 WAFFLES (DEPENDING ON WAFFLE IRON)

Oh my goodness, these waffles. Like, I can't. They are just so good. The trick here is that I took what normally would be a "blank canvas" of a batter and I've loaded it up with cinnamon, vanilla sugar, and a pinch of nutmeg. Toasted pecans, sorghum molasses, corn flour, and sea salt round out the flavor, making these delicious on their own or with a light drizzling of maple syrup. If you're feeling in the mood to be over-the-top, whip up the bananas Foster to smother on top. It's so easy and oh so decadent.

2 cups plain unsweetened plant-based milk

3 tablespoons vegetable oil

2 teaspoons sorghum molasses or regular molasses

1 teaspoon apple cider vinegar

1 teaspoon vanilla extract

1½ tablespoons vanilla sugar (see page 36)

1¾ cups all-purpose flour

¼ cup corn flour

1 teaspoon sea salt

1 tablespoon baking powder

1 tablespoon cornstarch

¼ teaspoon ground cinnamon

Dash freshly grated nutmeg

¼ cup chopped toasted pecans

Bananas Foster (page 231)

Vegan ice cream, to serve

1. Turn on your waffle maker and get it nice and hot.

2. In a large bowl, vigorously whisk the milk, oil, molasses, vinegar, vanilla extract, and vanilla sugar. In a separate bowl, sift together the flours, sea salt, baking powder, cornstarch, cinnamon, and nutmeg. Pour the milk mixture into the flour mixture and mix until smooth and incorporated. Fold in the pecans.

3. Spray a hefty amount of cooking oil on top and bottom of the waffle iron. Drizzle in the batter to cover the bottom mold. The cooking time will depend on your waffle iron, between 8 and 12 minutes, give or take.

4. Make the Bananas Foster as directed.

5. To serve, stack waffles on a plate and add a scoop of vegan vanilla ice cream. Drizzle the bananas Foster on top and make the world a better place.

lagniappe: *Try using a whisk to rapidly blend all your dry ingredients together. This will get rid of any clumps and eliminate the need to use a sifter.*

everything bagels

with all the fixings

MAKES 8 BAGELS

Growing up, my best friend, Alex, and her mother, Nina, loved making homemade bagels. Soft and tender, with a perfectly crispy crust, they were incredible, and I quickly realized the huge difference between homemade and store-bought bagels. Nina, Alex, and her sisters all chipped in to prepare the glorious spread of toppings and garnishes: almond cream cheese, thinly sliced shallots, roasted red peppers, capers, freshly cracked black pepper, sliced tomatoes, and loads of fresh herbs from the garden—obviously, they don't play. Below you will find the recipe, and please note that this is a *weekend* project as it can be a bit labor intensive. The bagels might not come out perfectly the first time, but you'll get the hang of it—practice makes perfect with this one. It only makes sense to dedicate this recipe to Nina and Alex. Thank you both for teaching me that the most important ingredient in a recipe is love.

1 tablespoon good olive oil, plus more for greasing the bowl and brushing

2¼ teaspoons active dry yeast

5 teaspoons + 2 teaspoons sugar

1¼ cups warm filtered water

2 teaspoons + 1 tablespoon sea salt

3⅓ cups bread flour (yes, bread flour—no substitutions)

2 teaspoons baking soda

Desired seasonings: sesame seeds, caraway seeds, poppy seeds, dried onion, dried garlic, etc.

Almond cream cheese, for serving

1. Coat a large mixing bowl with olive oil. In a second large mixing bowl, combine the yeast, 5 teaspoons of the sugar, and the water. Mix well. Let bloom for 7 to 10 minutes to make sure the yeast is active. Add the olive oil and 2 teaspoons of the sea salt. Mix well. Add the flour and mix until incorporated.

2. Plop the mixture onto a lightly floured counter and dust your hands with flour as well. Knead for 10 to 15 minutes, forming a ball of dough. During this process, the dough will be sticky. Feel free to sprinkle a light dusting of flour on top of the dough and the counter to help. If your hands become too sticky to continue kneading, take a break to wash them, re-dust them with flour, and go back at it. You want to keep the dough moist, so try not to add more than an additional ¼ cup of flour throughout the kneading process, otherwise the dough will become too dense. Once the dough holds together nicely and becomes springy (forming back toward you), it is ready.

recipe continues

recipe continued from previous page

3. Add the dough to the oil-coated bowl and then flip it, coating it evenly with oil. Cover with plastic wrap or a cloth and let rise in a warm spot until it doubles in size, about 1 hour, depending on the room's temperature.

4. Preheat the oven to 425°F. Line two baking sheets with parchment paper.

5. Once the dough has risen, punch it down and form it back into a smooth ball. Separate the dough into 8 equal pieces and roll them into cute little balls. Poke a hole in the center of each ball with your pointer finger, then pinch the hole all the way through and begin to shape them, tucking the dough underneath as you pinch through the hole (you want to create a doughnut shape with a smooth top). Place them on a baking sheet and let them rise for 10 minutes.

6. In a large pot, combine 5 quarts (20 cups) of water, the baking soda, the remaining 2 teaspoons sugar, and the remaining 1 tablespoon salt and bring to a boil. Place no more than 4 bagels into the pot at a time and poach them for 6 minutes, flipping them halfway through (3 minutes on each side). Remove and place them on a baking sheet. Repeat this step until all the bagels are poached.

7. Brush them with olive oil and sprinkle them with your favorite toppings. Bake until they are golden brown, about 20 minutes. Serve immediately with cream cheese.

my father's hash browns

SERVES 4

My father always made me hash browns growing up. I remember him dicing up potatoes into small squares, boiling them until tender, and crisping them up with loads of onions, garlic, black pepper, and sweet bell peppers. I've updated his recipe and added shallots, because I love their earthy sweetness. I prefer to use russet potatoes for hash browns because they have a firm, starchy texture. When you are chopping the potatoes, the goal is to cut the pieces around the same size so that they cook fast and evenly. A sprinkling of fresh herbs and a side of ketchup makes these really pop.

2 tablespoons vegetable oil

½ cup diced onions

1 pound russet potatoes, peeled, cut into ½-inch cubes, and boiled until tender

2 tablespoons diced garlic

2 tablespoons diced bell pepper (any color)

1 teaspoon rice vinegar

1 tablespoon nutritional yeast

½ teaspoon sea salt, or to taste

½ teaspoon freshly cracked black pepper, or to taste

Chopped fresh chives or green onion, for garnish

Ketchup, for serving

Favorite hot sauce (optional)

1. In a large cast-iron skillet, heat the oil over medium heat. Add the onions and cook for about 5 minutes to give them a head start. Add the potatoes and cook, stirring frequently, until the potatoes begin to brown nicely on the sides, about 10 minutes.

2. Once the potatoes are crispy, throw in the garlic, bell pepper, vinegar, nutritional yeast, sea salt, and black pepper. Mix well. Cook for an additional 5 minutes, stirring constantly so the garlic doesn't burn. Season with more salt and pepper, if desired.

3. Transfer to a bowl and sprinkle on the chives. Serve with ketchup and maybe some hot sauce if you're feeling sassy.

lagniappe: *I always use my trusty cast-iron skillet for this recipe, as it's naturally nonstick. If you don't have one, use a nonstick skillet or you may run into a sticky situation.*

crispy tofu breakfast sandwich

MAKES 4 SANDWICHES

Is it just me or does the thought of a breakfast sandwich excite you? I'm talking a deep excitement in your soul. There's something so satisfying about eating a warm breakfast in a handheld vessel. Of course, there are many different variations to play with, but this is how I roll. I've added a level of complexity with a hollandaise aioli that's bursting with flavor and richness. The combination of the sulfur-containing kala namak salt with ripe avocado and crispy rounds of tofu provides not only the flavor but also the richness and texture of a fried egg. The shiitake bacon contributes a classic smoky and salty crunch we all love on a breakfast sandwich. If desired, add a few slices of red onion and peppery arugula for a pop of color and flavor. If you're having a brunch, you can have all of these ingredients prepared and ready to assemble. Your guests will love you for it. Promise.

⅓ cup vegan butter, softened

2 tablespoons vegan mayo

2 tablespoons nutritional yeast

1 teaspoon mellow white miso or chickpea miso

1 tablespoon fresh lemon juice

¼ teaspoon white pepper

¼ teaspoon cayenne pepper

Dash ground turmeric

Drizzle of vegetable oil

1 block extra-firm tofu, sliced into ½-inch-thick slabs, patted dry

Kala namak salt

Freshly cracked black pepper

4 English muffins, gluten-free if desired

1 ripe avocado, sliced

Shiitake Bacon (page 254)

2 cups arugula (optional)

Thinly sliced red onion, for topping

1. **Prepare the hollandaise aioli:** In a small bowl, mix together the softened butter, mayo, nutritional yeast, miso, lemon juice, white pepper, cayenne pepper, and turmeric. Set aside.

2. In a large skillet, heat a drizzle of oil over medium heat. Add the tofu, spaced out, and cook until browned on each side, about 5 minutes per side. Transfer to a plate and sprinkle a dusting of kala namak and freshly cracked pepper on top.

3. To assemble the sandwiches, lightly toast the muffins. Spread on a layer of the aioli. Then add the avocado, bacon, tofu, arugula, if using, and onions. Spread some more aioli on the top bun and place it on top. Enjoy.

lagniappe: *If you want a fancier presentation, you can style the sandwich open-faced and use a squirt bottle to drizzle the hollandaise aioli artfully on top.*

garlic cheese grits casserole

with crunchy corn topping

SERVES 4 TO 6

The combination of garlic and cheese in grits has become a Southern classic, so I'm happy to share this vegan rendition with all of you. The first time I ever made this dish was when I was in high school, so it's a bit of a nostalgic throwback for me. I remember thinking to myself how fun it would be to have three different textures of corn in a dish: corn grits with fresh corn kernels and crunchy corn chips crumbled on top. And so, this casserole came to be! Feel free to make it ahead and keep it tightly covered in the fridge. When ready to serve, simply pop it in the oven to heat, then garnish.

---

4 cups filtered water

¼ cup vegan butter

¼ cup minced garlic

Dash cayenne pepper (optional)

½ teaspoon sweet paprika

1 ½ teaspoons sea salt, or to taste

½ teaspoon freshly cracked black pepper, or to taste

1 cup white heirloom corn grits

1 cup vegan cheddar-style cheese, shredded (about one 7-ounce pack)

1 cup corn kernels

½ cup crumbled corn chips, or to taste

Chopped green onions, for garnish

1. Preheat the oven to 350°F.

2. In a pot, combine the water, the butter, garlic, cayenne, if using, paprika, salt, and pepper and bring to a rapid boil.

3. Add the grits to the pot slowly, whisking to avoid clumping. Reduce to low heat and cook, stirring constantly, until thick and creamy, about 10 minutes. Remove from the heat and fold in the cheese and corn kernels. At this point, taste a little bit and season with salt and pepper.

4. Transfer to a 9 × 13-inch baking dish and bake for 20 minutes.

5. Let stand for 10 minutes before serving. Garnish with the corn chips and green onions.

lagniappe: *When it comes to corn, I always source the highest quality I can find: heirloom corn grits, organic frozen corn kernels, and non-GMO corn chips. For this recipe, look for the organic Frito-style chip.*

angelica kitchen's fluffy cornbread

SERVES 8

This cornbread recipe comes from my all-time favorite vegan restaurant, Angelica Kitchen. Although the establishment closed its doors in 2017, AK has a legacy that is untouchable. Sourcing only the best, organic produce and staying true to creating the healthiest of dishes, Angelica Kitchen served New York City for more than forty years! Incredible. I was lucky enough to work there for a short while as a server, and I am even luckier to be friends with the owner, Leslie, to this day. She was kind enough to grant me permission to use this recipe in my book, so here it is, one of my favorite items on their menu: their fluffy cornbread. It's light and moist, with a touch of sweetness from maple syrup. This recipe is a dedication to Angelica, for how much it taught and inspired me to eat food that truly nourishes my body and my mind.

1 cup finely ground cornmeal
½ cup whole-wheat pastry flour
½ cup unbleached white flour
2 teaspoons baking powder
¼ cup minced green onions
1 cup soy milk
¼ cup olive oil
¼ cup maple syrup
½ teaspoon sea salt

1. Preheat the oven to 350°F. Oil an 8- to 10-inch round ovenproof glass dish or cast-iron skillet.

2. In a large bowl, whisk together the cornmeal, flours, baking powder, and green onions. In a separate bowl, combine the soy milk, olive oil, maple syrup, and sea salt. Combine the wet and dry ingredients. Mix thoroughly with a wooden spoon. Do not overmix.

3. Pour into the oiled baking dish and bake until a toothpick comes out clean, about 25 minutes. Let cool for about 10 minutes, then slice into wedges and serve.

lagniappe: *This cornbread is absolutely divine with a thick layer of Angelica's Miso Tahini Spread. The restaurant was known for using all-natural ingredients in the most delicious way possible, and this spread was a perfect example. To make it, simply combine ⅓ cup mellow white miso, ½ cup filtered water, and 1⅓ cups tahini in a small bowl and mix together until smooth. Perfection!*

sausage biscuits

with jelly

MAKES 8 LARGE OR 12 SMALL BISCUIT SANDWICHES

Growing up in the South, the sausage biscuit was a popular breakfast. Oftentimes, we would smear a hefty amount of jelly onto each side of a biscuit before sandwiching the sausage patty in the middle. I recommend sweet pepper, strawberry, or grape jelly—the sweetness pairs perfectly with the salty, savory patty.

My drop biscuits are perfect for this recipe because they are super quick and easy to make, and they are light, fluffy, and buttery as all get-out. The sausage is what all of your childhood dreams are made of . . . meaty, savory, and unbelievably delicious. The key ingredient is the pearled barley, a chewy grain that plumps up when cooked—it replicates the texture of sausage. That, combined with loads of seasonings and spices, vital wheat gluten, and mashed chickpeas magically creates a sausagelike flavor and texture when cooked together. Once the patties are baked, grill them with a little vegan butter until they are crispy and they'll be ready for your sandwich.

drop biscuits

2¾ cups all-purpose flour

1½ tablespoons baking powder

¼ teaspoon baking soda

1 teaspoon sea salt

1 teaspoon sugar

2 tablespoons nutritional yeast

3 tablespoons cold vegan butter, plus some, melted, for brushing

2 tablespoons unmelted refined coconut oil

1¼ cups very cold plain almond or soy milk

assembly

¾ cup desired jelly

12 Barley Sausage patties (recipe follows)

1. Preheat the oven to 475°F and line one large or two small baking sheets with parchment paper.

2. Combine the flour, baking powder, baking soda, salt, sugar, and nutritional yeast in a large bowl. Using a whisk, vigorously mix the mixture, fluffing everything together and removing any clumps.

3. Add the cold butter and coconut oil. Using a fork or pastry cutter, cut in the butter until you are left with a crumbly texture. Pour in the milk and mix until just combined, making sure to get the dry bits at the bottom of the bowl.

4. Using an ice cream scoop, transfer 8 to 12 mounds of dough onto the prepared baking sheet(s). Bake for 15 to 20 minutes, until just the tops are slightly golden. Remove and brush with melted vegan butter.

5. Spread about 1 tablespoon of jelly onto each side of the biscuit and place a sausage patty in the middle.

recipe and ingredients continue

recipe continued from previous page

barley sausage

One 15-ounce can chickpeas (*not* drained)

1 cup sliced cremini mushrooms

¼ cup roughly chopped garlic

¼ cup nutritional yeast

2½ tablespoons chopped fennel seeds

2 tablespoons chopped fresh rosemary or 1 tablespoon dried

2 teaspoons garlic powder

2 teaspoons onion powder

2 teaspoons ground sage

1½ teaspoons sea salt, or to taste

½ teaspoon freshly cracked black pepper, or to taste

½ teaspoon dried oregano

½ teaspoon dried thyme

2½ tablespoons tamari, plus some for brushing

1 teaspoon liquid smoke

1 tablespoon vegan Worcestershire sauce

1 tablespoon mellow white miso or chickpea miso

2 teaspoons whole-grain mustard

½ cup peanut oil

¼ cup red wine

2 cups cooked pearled barley (from 1 cup uncooked)

2½ cups vital wheat gluten

1 cup water

Vegan butter, for cooking

1. **Make the breakfast sausage:** Preheat the oven to 350°F. Set out two 9 × 13-inch baking dishes for the sausage patties.

2. In a food processor, combine the chickpeas plus liquid, mushrooms, garlic, nutritional yeast, fennel seeds, rosemary, garlic powder, onion powder, sage, sea salt, pepper, oregano, thyme, tamari, liquid smoke, Worcestershire, miso, mustard, peanut oil, and red wine. Blend until smooth.

3. Transfer the mixture to a bowl. Stir in the barley and mix well. Slowly add the vital wheat gluten. Mix well. Once everything is incorporated, use your hands to knead the dough until it becomes springy. Gently pull apart the dough. When it has a stringy texture, it is ready.

4. Scoop out ¼ cup of the mixture and shape a sausage patty with your hands. Place in a baking dish. Repeat this step until all the patties are formed. Pour ½ cup of water into each baking dish over the patties, double wrap tightly with foil, and bake for 1 hour. Remove the foil, flip the patties, and bake for an additional 15 minutes, rotating the pans to ensure even cooking.

5. To finish, add a small amount of vegan butter (about 1 teaspoon per patty) to a large skillet and bring to medium heat. Brush a small amount of tamari (about ½ teaspoon per patty) on each side and add to the skillet. Cook for 1 or 2 minutes on each side until browned and crispy.

lagniappe: *One batch of the sausage patties makes about 20 servings, so you'll have some left over. If tightly covered, they keep in the fridge for 1 week and they freeze beautifully for up to 2 months. Try serving these patties with my Sautéed Collard Greens (page 198) and Garlic Cheese Grits Casserole (page 54) for an all-star breakfast.*

golden garlic biscuits

MAKES 12 BISCUITS

These biscuits are what they serve in heaven, right when you arrive at the gate—the most perfect garlic biscuits. If you aren't familiar with what I'm referring to, let me paint a picture: golden, crispy outside, soft and moist inside, a pop of garlic flavor with a slight cheesy tang, and little specks of green from chopped fresh parsley. The coconut yogurt mixed with your favorite plant-based milk creates a thick and creamy vegan buttermilk, which makes these biscuits moist and rich. The only problem? You can't eat just one.

¾ cup vegan butter

½ cup plain coconut yogurt

½ cup plain unsweetened plant-based milk

2 tablespoons minced garlic (use a Microplane)

1 tablespoon chopped fresh parsley

2 cups all-purpose flour

1 tablespoon baking powder

1 teaspoon garlic powder

1 teaspoon nutritional yeast

½ teaspoon sea salt

¼ teaspoon baking soda

Pinch sugar

1. Preheat the oven to 500°F and grease a 9 × 13-inch pan.

2. Roughly chop the butter and add to a small bowl. In a separate small bowl, whisk together the yogurt, milk, garlic, and parsley. Place *both* bowls in the freezer. In a large bowl, sift together the flour, baking powder, garlic powder, nutritional yeast, salt, baking soda, and sugar.

3. After the butter and wet ingredients are nice and cold (about 10 minutes), take them out. Add the butter to the flour mixture and mix with a fork, quickly breaking up and dispersing the butter into small chunks. Don't use your hands! Pour in the wet ingredients and mix until just incorporated.

4. Using a spoon or ice cream scoop, distribute the batter into 12 even mounds of dough (two rows of 6) in the prepared pan, leaving only a small amount of room in between the mounds (when baking, they will touch and help one another rise). Bake until the tops are golden brown, about 15 minutes.

lagniappe: *To make these over the top, sprinkle a bit of your favorite vegan cheese on the biscuits before baking. Totally not required, but life will be a little bit better if you do.*

blueberry pecan muffins

MAKES 18 MUFFINS

Blueberry picking has always been a favorite pastime for me and I can honestly say I enjoy it just as much as an adult as I did as a young boy. There's nothing quite like plucking off juicy ripe blueberries, warmed by the sun. My mama and I created this vegan version of a classic blueberry muffin recipe after we went blueberry picking one summer afternoon. She suggested that we put toasted pecan meal in the batter to add a butteriness to the muffins. I suggested that we throw in some orange and lemon zest for a tangy depth of flavor. This is what we came up with.

1 cup raw pecans

2½ cups all-purpose flour

2 tablespoons baking powder

1 tablespoon cornstarch

1¼ teaspoons sea salt

1 cup vanilla sugar (see page 36) or regular sugar, plus some for topping

1 teaspoon grated lemon zest

1 teaspoon grated orange zest

1 tablespoon vanilla extract

⅛ teaspoon almond extract

1½ cups full-fat coconut milk (13.5-ounce can)

¼ cup coconut oil, melted

¼ cup fresh lemon juice

¾ cup blueberries

1. Preheat the oven to 350°F.

2. Spread the pecans on a baking sheet and bake until toasted, about 10 minutes. Remove and let cool.

3. Increase the oven temperature to 375°F. Line muffin tin(s) with paper liners for 18 muffins.

4. In large bowl, sift together the flour, baking powder, cornstarch, and salt. In a food processor, combine the toasted pecans, sugar, lemon zest, and orange zest. Pulse intermittently until the mixture has a sandy texture. Halfway through pulsing, use a spatula to scrape the bottom and the sides. Mix this mixture into the flour mixture.

5. In a separate bowl, whisk together the vanilla extract, almond extract, coconut milk, coconut oil, and lemon juice. Whisk until smooth and fluffy. Pour the wet mixture into the dry mixture and mix gently with a spoon. Do not overmix!

6. Using a regular-sized ice cream scoop, scoop the batter into the muffin cups to fill the liners, leaving some room at the top until evenly distributed. Push 4 or 5 blueberries into each muffin. Sprinkle with sugar and bake until a toothpick comes out clean and the top edges are nicely browned, 25 to 35 minutes (depending on climate).

4. Remove from the oven and let cool in the pan for 15 minutes, then remove from the pan to cool for 30 minutes.

lagniappe: *I prefer placing the blueberries on top of the batter once poured instead of mixing them in as this ensures that each muffin has the same amount of berries and makes them visually pleasing on top.*

lagniappe: *If you don't have a cast-iron skillet, you can use a baking dish (you won't have to heat it beforehand), but you'll be missing out on that crispy crust!*

skillet cornbread

with red onions

MAKES 2 TO 3 SMALLER SKILLETS OR ONE 9-INCH SKILLET

This is the kind of cornbread that I imagine when I think of the South. Not too sweet, crumbly, and rich in corn flavor. My father taught me to always doctor up the batter with fresh corn kernels and sautéed onions and garlic. Some people add wheat flour to their cornbread, some use only cornmeal. For this go-'round, and because there is already a fluffy cornbread recipe a few pages back, I wanted to include a more old-school variation made with coarse, stone-ground yellow cornmeal that's cooked in a traditional cast-iron skillet. Preheating the skillet and melting butter all around the bottom and the edges before adding the batter creates a golden, crispy crust. A few slices of red onion on top provides an elegant finish.

2 cups coarse, stone-ground yellow cornmeal

1 teaspoon sea salt

1 teaspoon sugar

Dash cayenne pepper

½ teaspoon baking powder

½ teaspoon baking soda

1 tablespoon olive oil

1 cup diced onion

3 tablespoons diced garlic

½ cup fresh or frozen corn kernels

2 tablespoons chopped chives or green onions

⅓ cup vegetable oil

⅓ plant-based yogurt

⅓ cup plain unsweetened plant-based milk

Vegan butter, for the skillet

¼ small red onion, thinly sliced, for garnish

1. Preheat the oven to 450°F and place the desired skillet (s) in the oven until piping-hot.

2. In large mixing bowl, add the cornmeal, sea salt, sugar, cayenne pepper, baking powder, and baking soda. Using a whisk, combine the mixture, breaking up any clumps. Set aside.

3. Heat the olive oil in a medium skillet over medium-high heat and add the onion and garlic. Sauté for about 7 minutes, until soft and tender. Add the onion mixture, corn kernels, and chives to the cornmeal mixture. Mix well. Pour in the oil, yogurt, and milk. Stir until just combined.

4. Remove the skillet(s) carefully from the oven and add a small scoop of vegan butter. Swirl around and watch the butter sizzle. Transfer the batter to the skillet(s) and spread into an even layer. Delicately sprinkle on some red onion and bake for 20 minutes. Serve immediately.

lagniappe: *To jazz this recipe up even more, try adding some thinly sliced jalapenos or crushed pink peppercorns on top. I like to bring this cornbread to the table to serve as is and cut it straight out of the skillet.*

CHAPTER 2

—

snacks,
drinks &
appetizers

creole chex mix

SERVES 12

Now *this* is childhood, people. Well, at least for me it is. One of my earliest memories of this delectable snack was when my friend's mom dropped off some on my family's front porch. The doorbell rang, and as we opened the front door to see a minivan drive off in the distance, we noticed a small Chinese takeout container, with a little Christmas card, left behind. To our delight, when we picked up the container to take a look, we saw it was filled with a snack mix still warm from the oven. The buttery, toasty smell wafted out of the container as we immediately started shoveling handfuls into our mouths. Over the years, my version has become a bit more complex compared to the original, but for good reason. Crunchy cereal grains tossed with classic Creole spices, savory tamari, buttery pecans, and sweet cashews make for an addictively good snack. You can certainly halve this recipe if you would like, but I assure you that you'll be pissed if you do so. Don't make me say I told you so! Major bonus points for delivering this warm to a friend.

---

6 cups Chex-style cereal

1 cup raw pecans, roughly chopped

1 cup raw cashews, roughly chopped

½ cup olive oil

1½ tablespoons tamari or soy sauce

1½ tablespoons vegan Worcestershire sauce

1 teaspoon rice vinegar

⅓ cup nutritional yeast

1 tablespoon dried garlic pieces (see lagniappe below)

1 tablespoon dried onion pieces (see lagniappe below)

1 tablespoon onion powder

1 tablespoon garlic powder

1 teaspoon dried oregano

1 teaspoon dried parsley

1. Preheat the oven to 250°F. Line two large baking sheets with parchment paper.

2. In a very large bowl, combine the cereal, pecans, and cashews. In a separate bowl, whisk together the olive oil, tamari, Worcestershire, and vinegar. Slowly drizzle one-third of the mixture over the cereal mixture. Using a large spoon or spatula, delicately toss the mixture. Repeat until the wet ingredients are thoroughly incorporated into the cereal and nuts (coating everything thoroughly will ensure that the dry seasonings stick to each and every piece).

3. In a separate bowl, mix together the nutritional yeast, dried garlic, dried onion, onion powder, garlic powder, oregano, parsley, thyme, paprika, sugar, cayenne, and salt, if using. Mix well with a fork. Sprinkle one-fourth on top of the cereal mixture. Gently toss. Repeat until all of the dry mixture is used. At this point, taste a little bit to see if it needs any salt. If so, sprinkle a little bit on top, mix, and repeat until you are

recipe and ingredients continue

1 teaspoon dried thyme

1 teaspoon sweet paprika

1 teaspoon sugar

¼ to ½ teaspoon cayenne
pepper, to taste

Sea salt, to taste (optional)

2 teaspoons toasted sesame oil

satisfied. Depending on the cereal and the Worcestershire you use, you may not need any at all, so just taste to see.

4. Divide the mixture in half, setting one-half aside. Using both baking sheets, spread the mixture into a thin, even layer. Bake for 1 hour, stirring every 15 minutes and switching racks after 30 minutes. Remove from the oven, let cool, and transfer to a large bowl.

5. Bake the second half of the mixture as above. Once cooled, add it to the bowl with the first batch. Drizzle 1 teaspoon of the sesame oil on top and toss. Repeat with the remaining 1 teaspoon oil (it provides a unique butteriness). Keep in an airtight jar for up to 3 weeks.

lagniappe: *You can find the dried onion and garlic pieces in the section where they sell salad toppings. I like to use a blend of rice, corn, and wheat Chex cereal, but you can stick to one variety if that's all you can find.*

roasted pumpkin seeds

SERVES 2 TO 4

One of my favorite field trips as a young boy was going to the pumpkin patch, and that image of clusters of large, bright orange pumpkins scattered throughout a vast field will forever pop into my mind when the first cool breeze of fall arrives. Now, if I remember correctly, the goal of the trip was to bring home a beautiful pumpkin to carve for Halloween. But my favorite part, or rather result, was when we roasted the abundance of leftover pumpkin seeds.

This variation is cheesy and salty, with a touch of spice. The best part is having your whole home smelling absolutely scrumptious while they bake. I'd say they'd be good sprinkled on top of a salad, but they have honestly never lasted that long for me. Good luck!

1½ cups whole pumpkin seeds, rinsed and dried

1½ tablespoons nutritional yeast

1 tablespoon olive oil

1 tablespoon tamari

1 teaspoon rice vinegar

¼ teaspoon sea salt, or to taste

¼ teaspoon freshly cracked black pepper, or to taste

Dash cayenne pepper

Dash sweet paprika

½ tablespoon toasted sesame oil

1. Preheat the oven to 300°F. Line a large baking sheet with parchment paper.

2. In a small bowl, combine the pumpkin seeds, nutritional yeast, olive oil, tamari, vinegar, salt, black pepper, cayenne, and paprika and mix well.

3. Spread the seeds in an even layer on the baking sheet. Bake for 30 minutes. Toss, then bake until golden brown and crispy, 20 to 30 minutes longer.

4. Remove from the oven, drizzle with the toasted sesame seed oil, and carefully toss. Let cool for 10 minutes before enjoying, as they will crisp up even more. Keep them stored in a tightly sealed container for up to a few days.

cajun boiled peanuts

SERVES 6

If you've never had boiled peanuts, you're missing out. There's a simple satisfaction in peeling the shell off with your mouth and scooping the tender peanuts out with your teeth. A classic recipe and tradition in the South, you can find boiled peanuts at every local farmers' market and even many gas stations. Most of the time, they are seasoned with a whole bunch of sketchy ingredients such as MSG, preservatives, and an insane amount of sodium. As it turns out, this makes them incredibly flavorful. But you don't need all of that nonsense to make a delicious boiled peanut. Loaded with herbs and spices, this recipe is proof that you won't be able to just eat one. You can easily make this recipe in a large pot, but it's super-duper easy to throw them into a slow cooker for a few hours. Set it and forget it, people.

---

1 pound raw, green peanuts

16 cups filtered water

3 tablespoons Old Bay seasoning

5 large dried bay leaves

2 tablespoons fresh lemon juice

2 tablespoons tamari or coconut aminos

2 tablespoons nutritional yeast

1½ tablespoons onion powder

1½ tablespoons garlic powder

1 tablespoon ume plum vinegar

2 teaspoons sugar

1 teaspoon crushed red pepper flakes

1 teaspoon black peppercorns

½ teaspoon sweet paprika

1. Rinse the peanuts well. Add them to a slow cooker or large pot with the water, the Old Bay, bay leaves, lemon juice, tamari, nutritional yeast, onion powder, garlic powder, vinegar, sugar, pepper flakes, black peppercorns, and paprika. Mix well.

2. If using a slow cooker, cook, covered, for at least 3 hours on low, stirring occasionally. If cooking on the stovetop, bring the peanuts to a boil and reduce the heat to low. Cook for 3 hours, partially covered, stirring occasionally. The water will reduce while cooking, so every so often, add water when needed to keep the peanuts covered (about once per hour).

3. Once done, drain and serve hot or cold. To store in the fridge, place the peanuts plus liquid to cover in an airtight jar for up to 1 week.

lagniappe: *Make sure the peanuts you buy are labeled as "raw" or "green." You can sometimes find them fresh at the farmers' market or dried at your local grocery store. If not, check the nearest Asian market, as they often will have them as well.*

ginger-mint limeade

SERVES 4

There's nothing quite as refreshing as a cool glass of lemonade on a hot Mississippi day. When I was a little boy, we would always have a lemonade stand and sell a cup for $1. That flashback came to me one day recently when I was working in the yard. My shirt was sticking to me and my mouth was craving something juicy and refreshing. I knew in my heart an ice-cold glass of lemonade would do the trick, but I decided to change things up and make something a tad more interesting. Instead of using only lemons, I added limes to the mix along with fresh mint and ginger. Instead of using refined sugar, I used maple syrup. It's a ridiculously refreshing beverage reminiscent of classic Southern-style lemonade, but a bit more healthy and sophisticated.

6 cups filtered water

2 to 3 juicy lemons

5 to 6 juicy limes, plus slices for garnish

2 cups packed fresh mint sprigs, plus some for garnish

½ cup maple syrup

6 tablespoons chopped fresh ginger (about 3 ounces)

1 cup ice

1. Line a fine-mesh strainer with a large piece of cheesecloth, folded over once. There should be enough excess cheesecloth hanging around the strainer to pull up the sides and squeeze the mixture.

2. In a high-powered blender, combine the water, lemon juice, lime juice, mint, maple syrup, ginger, and ice. Blend on high until smooth. Pour into the cheesecloth-lined sieve. Once most of the liquid has been strained, gently pull the cheesecloth up on each side and twist and squeeze gently, squeezing out the remaining liquid.

3. To serve, fill glasses with ice and pour the limeade over. Garnish with lime slices and fresh mint sprigs. Serve with straws.

lagniappe: *I highly recommend making a large batch of this for a lunch or dinner party, as it is quite impressive sitting in a beautiful jar on the counter! Make sure to load it up with lemon and lime slices and loads of fresh mint sprigs. It will be bursting with color. This also makes for a great cocktail base. Simply add your desired spirit.*

lavender & meyer lemon pop

MAKES 2 HIGHBALL COCKTAILS

Freshly muddled lavender and fresh lemon is a dream come true! *Especially* when it's Meyer lemons. Their robust and earthy juice is sweeter than traditional lemons. My aunt in Baton Rouge has a tree that's always full of fruit in the wintertime. She always hooks it up. And I simply can't get enough. Now imagine muddling that with lavender? Forget it! I grow my own lavender, but you can most likely find some at your local farmers' market or go-to garden store. You can leave out the vodka for a refreshing drink, but what's the fun in that? Add the vodka, call a friend, take a bubble bath.

---

1 teaspoon sugar

1 tablespoon packed fresh lavender leaves, plus more for garnish

1 large Meyer lemon, sliced into wheels

Ice cubes

2 ounces fresh Meyer lemon juice

3 ounces vodka

Plain sparkling water

1. In a cocktail shaker, combine the sugar, lavender, and 2 lemon wheels and muddle. Add the ice, lemon juice, and vodka. Shake well.

2. Strain into two ice-filled Collins glasses. Top each with sparkling water and garnish with lavender flowers and a fresh lemon wheel. Drink.

lagniappe: *Meyer lemons are becoming increasingly more popular and available in traditional grocery stores. They have a thinner skin compared to a traditional lemon, and their color is a cross between yellow and orange. I guess that's because that's precisely what a Meyer lemon is, a cross between a lemon and an orange!*

satsuma whiskey cider

MAKES 8 CUPS APPLE CIDER AND MULTIPLE COCKTAILS

This cocktail is almost *too* easy to drink. You know, the kind that can get you into trouble. First, you simply make a killer mulled cider by infusing apple juice with loads of spices and fresh ginger. Then you mix that with some buttery whiskey in a glass and garnish with a squeeze of fresh satsuma. Like I said, trouble.

mulled cider

8 cups high-quality pure, unsweetened apple juice

2 cinnamon sticks

1 tablespoon chopped fresh ginger

½ teaspoon whole cloves

¼ teaspoon ground allspice

¼ teaspoon freshly grated nutmeg

for serving

Ice, preferably one large cube

Kentucky bourbon whiskey

4 to 5 small satsumas, sliced, plus some for garnish

1. **Make the mulled cider:** In a medium pot, combine the apple juice, cinnamon sticks, ginger, cloves, allspice, and nutmeg and bring to a boil. Reduce the heat and simmer for about 20 minutes. Once it smells fragrant and spicy, remove from the heat and let cool. Strain through a fine-mesh sieve into a jar. It will keep in the fridge for 1 to 2 weeks.

2. When ready to serve, add ice to the glass (bonus points for cute mason jars), along with one shot of whiskey. Pour in the mulled cider and squeeze in a slice of satsuma. Garnish with a fresh slice. Sip slowly and enjoy!

bloody mary

SERVES 10 TO 12

This popular cocktail may not be Southern, but Southerners *act* like it is. A brunch tradition, this tomato and vodka–based drink is a festive way to cure any hangover while also getting in your daily dose of vegetables. I love loading mine up with all the veggies I can get my hands on. My two major requirements are pickled okra and celery. Anything else is up to you. As for the base, I like using fresh horseradish for its refreshing kick (you can find it in the produce section of your grocery store); and the fresh lemon and lime juices help this mix shine like the sun.

32 ounces tomato juice (a 1-quart jar)

2 to 3 tablespoons grated fresh horseradish, to taste

½ teaspoon grated lemon zest

½ teaspoon grated lime zest

3 tablespoons fresh lemon juice

3 tablespoons fresh lime juice

2 tablespoons vegan Worcestershire sauce

1 tablespoon tamari

2 teaspoons Louisiana hot sauce

3 small garlic cloves, minced or Microplaned

2 stalks celery, chopped

2 tablespoons nutritional yeast

1 teaspoon smoked or sweet paprika, plus some for serving

1 teaspoon sugar

½ teaspoon sea salt, plus some for serving

Dash cayenne pepper

Freshly cracked black pepper, to taste

Lemon slices, for serving

Ice, for serving

Vodka, for serving

Pickled vegetables, for serving

1. **Make the Bloody Mary mix:** In a blender, combine all of the ingredients and blend until smooth. If you are serving immediately, transfer to a pitcher. If for later, transfer to a tightly sealed jar and keep in the fridge for up to 1 week.

2. When ready to serve, combine a small amount of sea salt and smoked paprika on a small plate and mix well. Rub a piece of lemon around a cocktail glass and dip into the salt mixture, coating the rim. Fill with ice and add one shot of vodka (or more if you've had a bad week). Top with Bloody Mary mix and stud in pickled vegetables of your choice.

lagniappe: *For a festive assortment of fixin's, hit up the olive bar at your grocery store for some great options. I love using roasted garlic cloves, sweet peppers, baby pickles, chipotle carrots—the more the merrier, honestly! Take advantage of what's done and ready to go.*

watermelon slushy

with Thai basil

SERVES 2 TO 4

I created this refreshing treat when I was living in Charleston, South Carolina. It was a hot-as-hell summer day, and my friend Franny came over and said she was craving a slushy. Instead of going to the gas station, I threw some frozen watermelon into the blender with some water and voilà! A homemade, refreshing slushy was born. Of course, I've added a few little touches to jazz it up for you guys. Feel free to push and pull this recipe in whatever direction you would like. Change the Thai basil to mint, switch out the lemon or lime with orange juice, add more agave, or take it out completely. It's really up to you and whatever you are craving at the moment.

¾ cup filtered water

5 cups frozen, ripe watermelon chunks

2 tablespoons fresh lemon or lime juice

2 to 4 tablespoons agave syrup, depending on sweetness desired

½ cup minced fresh Thai basil, plus some for garnish

In a blender, combine 1 cup of the frozen watermelon and the water. Blend until smooth. Add the rest of the watermelon, along with the lemon or lime juice, agave, if using, and basil. Blend again until smooth. Transfer to desired glasses and serve with a straw or spoon on a hot summer day. Garnish with fresh basil.

lagniappe: *Try sourcing a very ripe watermelon at your local farmers' market. The best way to determine if a watermelon is ripe is to knock it to see if it sounds hollow. Try holding it up to your ear to listen; it's fun. To freeze the watermelon, cut into slices, remove the rind and white parts, and cut into 2-inch chunks. Place in a tightly sealed container and keep in the freezer for up to a few months.*

fig & shallot tart

with roasted garlic almond spread

SERVES 8 TO 10

I've always been a sucker for the classic combination of juicy, sweet figs and a tangy, salty cheese. The only thing better is putting those ingredients on a crust with caramelized shallots and onions. If you're nervous about eating large chunks of onions and shallots, don't be. Once they caramelize, they become tender and incredibly sweet (of course, a touch of sugar helps!). The figs intensify in flavor as they bake, and their seeds provide a lovely crunch. I like using almonds for the cheese, as they provide a nice texture once blended, but you can use whatever nuts you like. This is the perfect appetizer for a dinner party, or serve it with a salad for lunch.

roasted garlic almond spread

2 heads garlic

Olive oil, for drizzling

¾ cup blanched almonds

½ cup filtered water

1½ tablespoons mellow white or chickpea miso

½ teaspoon grated lemon zest

1 tablespoon fresh lemon juice

1 teaspoon garlic powder

¼ teaspoon sea salt

1. **Make the roasted garlic almond spread:** Preheat the oven to 400°F. Line a baking sheet or cast-iron skillet with parchment paper.

2. With a sharp knife, cut the tops off each garlic head, just enough to reveal the tips of all the cloves. Drizzle with olive oil and roast them until golden brown and soft, 40 to 50 minutes, depending on garlic head size. Once cooled, you should be able to squeeze the cloves out easily. If not, pop them back in the oven until softer. Leave the oven on.

3. Squeeze the roasted garlic cloves into a food processor. Add the almonds, water, miso, lemon zest, lemon juice, garlic powder, and sea salt. Blend for 5 to 10 minutes, scraping down the sides as needed, until you are left with a thick, smooth paste. Set aside.

4. **Make the tarts:** Quarter the shallots and onions, leaving just enough of the white bottom cores to allow them to keep all of the layers intact. Place them on the baking sheet and toss with the sugar and drizzle with olive oil. Arrange the onions and shallots cut-side down and roast until the onions and

recipe and ingredients continue

recipe continued from previous page

tart

4 large shallots (about 6 ounces), peeled and rinsed

4 baby or small red onions (about 8 ounces), peeled and rinsed

3 teaspoons sugar, plus some for sprinkling

Olive oil, for drizzling

Two sheets frozen vegan puff pastry (one 17-ounce package), thawed

12 fresh figs, quartered

1 teaspoon sea salt

1 tablespoon balsamic vinegar

Fresh oregano or thyme leaves, for garnish

shallots are caramelized, 30 to 45 minutes. Remove from the oven and let cool. Leave the oven on.

5. Line two baking sheets with parchment paper. Sprinkle a dusting of flour onto a clean surface and use a rolling pin to gently roll out the thawed puff pastry squares into slightly longer rectangles (around 10 to 12 inches on the long side). This will allow more surface area for the toppings. If the dough feels thin, remember it is going to puff up!

6. Transfer each pastry sheet onto a lined baking sheet. Using a small knife, score a thin border around each piece of dough (about ½ inch in from the edges). Dividing evenly, spread the tarts with the almond spread. Arrange the onions, shallots, and figs beautifully on top and gently press them into the spread. Sprinkle each of the tarts with sea salt and sugar and drizzle with the balsamic vinegar.

7. Bake until the crust is golden brown, 20 to 30 minutes. Cut into small rectangles, garnish with fresh oregano or thyme leaves, and serve. Best if eaten immediately.

lagniappe: *You can make these tarts in advance and bake them when you are ready to serve. Simply assemble the tarts, cover them tightly with foil or plastic wrap, and keep in the fridge. Since the recipe makes two, feel free to pop one in the freezer so you have it ready to go when needed—just defrost it before baking.*

cheese straws

SERVES 8 TO 10

This right here is quintessential Mississippi: a piece of McCarty pottery with a cluster of delectable cheese straws. That's just how we roll here in the 'Sip! For those of you who don't know, McCarty is a family-owned Mississippi-based pottery company, and almost every home in the state proudly collects their pieces. You can identify them by their trademarked "river," a small black wavy line that represents the Mississippi River. My mother gave me this very piece in the photograph and you can clearly see the "river" line. Now, are you likely to see *vegan* cheese straws served on a piece of McCarty? Probably not, but we can totally change that! If you aren't familiar with cheese straws, they are sticks of savory shortbread dough made with butter and cheese. Most varieties have some cayenne pepper for a kick. I find that store-bought vegan cheddar cheese works just fine for this traditional recipe, with an additional cheesy boost from miso and tang from ume plum vinegar. They're so delicious, no one will notice or care that they're vegan. Trust.

---

1 cup vegan butter

1 cup shredded vegan cheddar-style cheese

¼ cup nutritional yeast

¼ cup mellow white miso or chickpea miso

¼ teaspoon cayenne pepper

1 teaspoon garlic powder

1 teaspoon onion powder

1 teaspoon ume plum vinegar

½ teaspoon ground turmeric

½ teaspoon sweet paprika

½ teaspoon sugar

1 cup all-purpose flour

1. Preheat the oven to 325°F. Line a baking sheet with parchment paper.

2. In a large bowl, with an electric mixer, combine all of the ingredients except the flour and beat until fluffy. Slowly mix in the flour while beating.

3. Fit a piping bag with a star tip and set in a container or large tall glass. Using a spatula, transfer the dough to the piping bag and squeeze straw shapes, about 4 inches in length, onto the lined baking sheet.

4. Bake until golden brown, about 20 minutes. Let cool for about 10 minutes and enjoy. These will store in a tightly sealed container for a few days but are best eaten immediately.

lagniappe: *If you have a cookie press, well then look at you go! That will work beautifully for this recipe so whip it out and skip the piping bag.*

fried pickles

SERVES 4 TO 6

I know what you might be thinking . . . fried pickles? Well, yup! Fried pickles! I grew up eating them and let me tell you, they're outrageously good. Tangy, salty, and crispy—and even more amazing dipped in a creamy Comeback Sauce (page 264) or my Zesty Ranch (page 263). So. Good. Traditionally, egg is used to help the batter stick, but I simply add a little pickle juice instead. It works perfectly. This recipe makes enough for a small group of people, but I could honestly kill this whole batch by myself. No shame.

batter

One 16-ounce jar hamburger pickle dill chips, drained

½ cup all-purpose flour

3 tablespoons pickle juice

2 tablespoons water

½ teaspoon sugar

coating

¾ cup all-purpose flour

3 tablespoons cornstarch

3 tablespoons nutritional yeast

1 teaspoon Old Bay seasoning

1 teaspoon sea salt

½ teaspoon freshly cracked black pepper

½ teaspoon cayenne pepper

½ teaspoon sweet paprika

for frying

A few cups peanut oil

for serving

Comeback Sauce (page 264)
Zesty Ranch (page 263)

1. **Make the batter:** In a bowl, mix together the pickles, flour, pickle juice, water, and sugar until the pickles are thoroughly coated with what looks like a glue.

2. **Make the coating:** In a separate bowl, mix together the flour, cornstarch, nutritional yeast, Old Bay, salt, black pepper, cayenne, and paprika. Add the pickles and toss them thoroughly with the dry mix.

3. **Fry the pickles:** Pour oil to reach three quarters of an inch into a large skillet or saucepan and heat over medium-high heat. Once hot, carefully place the breaded pickles into the oil. Fry until golden brown, 2 to 3 minutes. You do not need to flip.

4. Drain the pickles on a plate with a few sheets of paper towel and serve immediately, with your choice of sauce.

stuffed mushrooms

SERVES 6 TO 8

I didn't grow up eating mushrooms that often, but when I did, I loved them. Eventually, I realized that when I did have them it was because of my grandfather, Papa. He loved mushrooms, along with celery, my other favorite food. Therefore, these stuffed mushrooms are a tribute to him because I know he would have loved them. Using a spoon, you scoop out the insides of cremini mushrooms (stems and all). Then, you chop up the scooped-out mushrooms and add loads of spices, herbs, breadcrumbs, and vegan cheese. After packing the caps tightly with this flavorful filling and baking them in the oven, you are left with succulent, juicy, and incredibly tasty stuffed mushrooms.

5 tablespoons olive oil

4 tablespoons nutritional yeast, plus more for sprinkling

2 tablespoons tamari

½ teaspoon liquid smoke

1 pound cremini (baby bella) mushrooms, cleaned

¼ cup chopped garlic

1 shallot, minced

1½ cups breadcrumbs, plus more for sprinkling

1 cup diced vegan cheese

1 tablespoon chopped fresh oregano

1 tablespoon chopped fresh parsley

1 tablespoon chopped fresh sage

½ teaspoon freshly cracked black pepper

1. Preheat the oven to 400°F.

2. In a small bowl, whisk together 2 tablespoons of the olive oil, 2 tablespoons of the nutritional yeast, the tamari, and liquid smoke to make a marinade.

3. Stem the mushrooms and set the stems aside. Using a spoon, delicately scrape out the inside gills of the mushrooms to create an empty cavity for the stuffing. Rub the marinade on each mushroom cap and set aside.

4. Finely chop the mushrooms stems and add them to a bowl along with the remaining 3 tablespoons olive oil and the remaining 2 tablespoons nutritional yeast. Throw in the garlic, shallot, breadcrumbs, cheese, oregano, parsley, sage, and pepper. Mix well. Mound the filling into the mushrooms, piling it high! Don't be scared to pack it in.

5. Transfer the stuffed mushrooms to a baking sheet or cast-iron skillet and sprinkle with breadcrumbs and a tiny bit of nutritional yeast. Spray with cooking oil and bake until golden brown on top, 30 to 40 minutes. Enjoy!

lagniappe: *Try finding the biggest, most beautiful mushrooms that you can for this recipe. Any small ones in the bunch can be chopped up for the stuffing.*

happy crab cake bites

SERVES 10

These are just the cutest and most delicious little bite-size cakes, perfect for passing as an hors d'oeuvre or for serving as a dinner party appetizer. You can make the mixture ahead of time and bake them up when you are ready to serve. The shredded artichoke hearts have a texture similar to crabmeat, so I call these guys Happy Crab Cake Bites, because the crabs are left alone, unbothered, and not eaten. So they're happy. Get it?

cakes

2½ cups marinated artichoke hearts, drained and shredded or thinly sliced

1 cup cooked chickpeas, rinsed, drained, and mashed (not pureed)

1 cup panko breadcrumbs

½ cup minced onion

¼ cup minced celery

¼ cup minced red bell pepper

¼ cup minced green bell pepper

¼ cup thinly sliced green onions, plus some for garnish

¼ cup nutritional yeast

3 tablespoons vegan mayo

2 tablespoons chopped fresh parsley

2 tablespoons minced garlic

1 tablespoon red wine vinegar

2 teaspoons Old Bay seasoning

1 teaspoon sugar

1 teaspoon whole-grain mustard

1 teaspoon dried thyme, crushed with fingers

¼ teaspoon onion powder

¼ teaspoon sweet paprika

1. **Make the cakes:** Preheat the oven to 400°F and line a large baking sheet with parchment paper.

2. In a large bowl, mix together the artichoke hearts, mashed chickpeas, panko, onion, celery, bell peppers, green onions, nutritional yeast, mayo, parsley, garlic, vinegar, Old Bay, sugar, mustard, thyme, onion powder, and paprika until thoroughly incorporated. Cover and refrigerate for about 30 minutes. This will help the mixture combine for effective shaping.

3. **Make the coating:** In a separate bowl, combine the panko, olive oil, Old Bay, nutritional yeast, and pepper and mix well.

recipe and ingredients continue

recipe continued from previous page

coating

1¼ cups panko breadcrumbs

2 tablespoons olive oil

1 teaspoon Old Bay seasoning

1 teaspoon nutritional yeast

¼ teaspoon freshly cracked
   black pepper

for serving

Rémoulade (page 261)

Sliced green onions (optional)

4. Remove the cake mixture from the refrigerator and using about 2 tablespoons, shape into golf ball–size rounds with your hands. Over the bowl of coating, press the coating around the ball, then gently flatten the ball to create a small cake on the prepared baking sheet. Repeat this step until all of the cakes are formed.

5. Spray the cakes with cooking oil and bake for 30 minutes, or until golden brown. Transfer to a serving platter with a bowl of rémoulade and garnish with sliced green onions, if desired.

frito pie

with quick and easy chili

SERVES 4 TO 6

Growing up, I was always hanging out at the baseball field, usually to watch my sisters play softball. And by watching them play, I mean I was running around with boys in the ditches surrounding the park and eating all of the junk food they served at the concession stand. The parents ran the stand, usually the moms, so think big hair, loads of makeup, and shoulder pads. On the menu were hot dogs, hamburgers, nachos, jumbo pickles, candy, and, you guessed it, Frito pie. Salty, crunchy corn chips topped with savory chili and a creamy cheese sauce (okay, let's be real, nacho cheese). I don't know *who* thought of this ridiculous combination, but they were genius. Genius, I tell you! Please do yourself a favor and try this recipe immediately. Like, now.

cheese sauce

One 7-ounce package American-style vegan cheese slices, chopped

One 7-ounce package provolone-style vegan cheese slices, chopped

½ cup + 2 tablespoons plain unsweetened soy or almond milk

2 teaspoons nutritional yeast

1 tablespoon fresh lemon juice

Two 9-ounce bags Frito-style corn chips

4 to 6 cups Quick and Easy Chili (recipe follows) or 2 cans vegan chili

1 bunch green onions, thinly sliced

1 pint cherry tomatoes, halved or quartered

1. In a small pot, combine the cheeses, milk, nutritional yeast, and lemon juice and cook over medium heat, stirring frequently, until smooth and creamy, 10 to 15 minutes.

2. Place 1½ to 2 cups of the corn chips into each of 4 to 6 separate serving bowls. Scoop about 1 cup of the chili on top and drizzle with about ½ cup of the cheese sauce. Garnish with green onions and cherry tomatoes. Serve immediately, as the chips will get soggy.

recipe and ingredients continue

recipe continued from previous page

quick and easy chili

SERVES 6 TO 8

1 cup dried TVP (textured vegetable protein)

2 tablespoons nutritional yeast

1 tablespoon onion powder

1 tablespoon garlic powder

2 teaspoons chili powder

2 teaspoons ground cumin

1 teaspoon dried Mexican or regular oregano

½ teaspoon dried thyme

½ teaspoon sweet paprika

¼ teaspoon cayenne pepper (optional)

1 cup boiling water

2 tablespoons olive oil

1 large onion, chopped

¼ cup chopped garlic

½ cup red wine

1 teaspoon cornstarch

One 15-ounce can black or pinto beans, rinsed and drained

One 14.5-ounce can fire-roasted diced tomatoes

1 tablespoon rice vinegar

Sea salt and freshly cracked black pepper

1. In a bowl, combine the TVP, nutritional yeast, onion powder, garlic powder, chili powder, cumin, oregano, thyme, sweet paprika, and cayenne, if using, and mix well. Pour in the boiling water, mix well, and set aside to plump up the TVP.

2. In a large pot, heat the olive oil over medium heat. Add the onion and cook until tender and golden on the edges, about 10 minutes. Add the garlic, and continue to cook for an additional 5 minutes, stirring often to prevent burning. Add the TVP mixture. Cook, stirring constantly, for a good 5 minutes to toast all of the spices.

3. Add the red wine and deglaze the bottom of the pot, stirring well to scrape anything sticking to the bottom of the pot. In a separate bowl, mix together 1 cup filtered water and cornstarch until well blended. Add this along with the beans, tomatoes, and rice vinegar to the pot. Mix well and bring to a boil. Reduce the heat to low and give it a taste. Season with salt and pepper as desired.

garlic & herb bread

SERVES 4 TO 6

I'm a garlic bread fiend. I just can't get enough. Can you? Am I alone here? Didn't think so. Here we have a little garlic bread recipe done my way. I love packing in as many fresh herbs as possible—to the point where the buttery spread is bright green. If you have a garden or even a tiny bit of space outside of your apartment or fire escape for a few pots, try growing some lemon and lime basil. These varieties are bursting with citrusy and tangy flavor. I simply adore them. But feel free to play with any herbs that you can get your hands on. (I've provided a few different variations on the following page.) I like to throw in some lemon zest and lemon juice to give this recipe a bright little pop, too! Slather the herbed butter onto two halves of a loaf of crusty bread and wrap it tightly to bake it. This infuses the whole loaf of bread beautifully with deliciousness, while also allowing the garlic and shallots to become tender and sweet. Then separate the halves and bake butter-side up until crispy. Perfection.

1½ cups tightly packed fresh lime basil (see Variations)

1½ cups tightly packed fresh lemon or lime basil (see Variations)

1 cup vegan butter

½ cup chopped shallot (about 1 large)

½ cup chopped garlic (1 to 2 heads)

1 teaspoon grated lemon zest

3 tablespoons fresh lemon juice (about 2 lemons)

1½ teaspoons sea salt, or to taste

Freshly cracked black pepper

2 loaves ciabatta bread, cut lengthwise in half (like you would for a large sandwich)

1. Preheat the oven to 350°F.

2. In a small blender or food processor, combine the basil, vegan butter, shallot, garlic, lemon zest, lemon juice, salt, and pepper to taste. Blend until smooth.

3. Spread your desired amount of the butter on the cut sides of the halved loaves. Sandwich the halves together, buttered sides together, and tightly wrap each loaf with foil. Bake for about 20 minutes to infuse the bread with flavor. Remove from the oven, but leave the oven on.

4. Carefully, unwrap the bread and separate the halves. Using a bread knife, cut the halves into desired shapes or leave the halves whole. Cutting into smaller pieces will yield crispier bread, as there will be more surface to toast. Your choice!

5. Place the bread, herb butter–side facing up, on the baking sheet and bake until the edges are golden brown or you reach your desired crispiness, an additional 15 to 20 minutes. Serve immediately.

lagniappe: *You can store the herb butter tightly sealed in the fridge for a few weeks or, better yet, in the freezer for the wintertime when you do not have access to the glorious summer herbs.*

VARIATIONS

If you can't find fresh lemon or lime basil, try any of these easy variations of fresh herbs along with the remaining ingredients for the herb butter.

2 cups chopped sweet basil + 1 cup chopped fresh chives

—

½ cup chopped fresh oregano + ¼ cup chopped fresh thyme + 1 cup chopped fresh parsley

—

2 tablespoons chopped fresh rosemary + 1 cup chopped fresh chives + ½ cup chopped green onions

—

1 cup chopped fresh tarragon + 1 cup chopped fresh chives

—

1 cup chopped fresh parsley + 1 cup chopped fresh dill + 1 cup chopped fresh chives

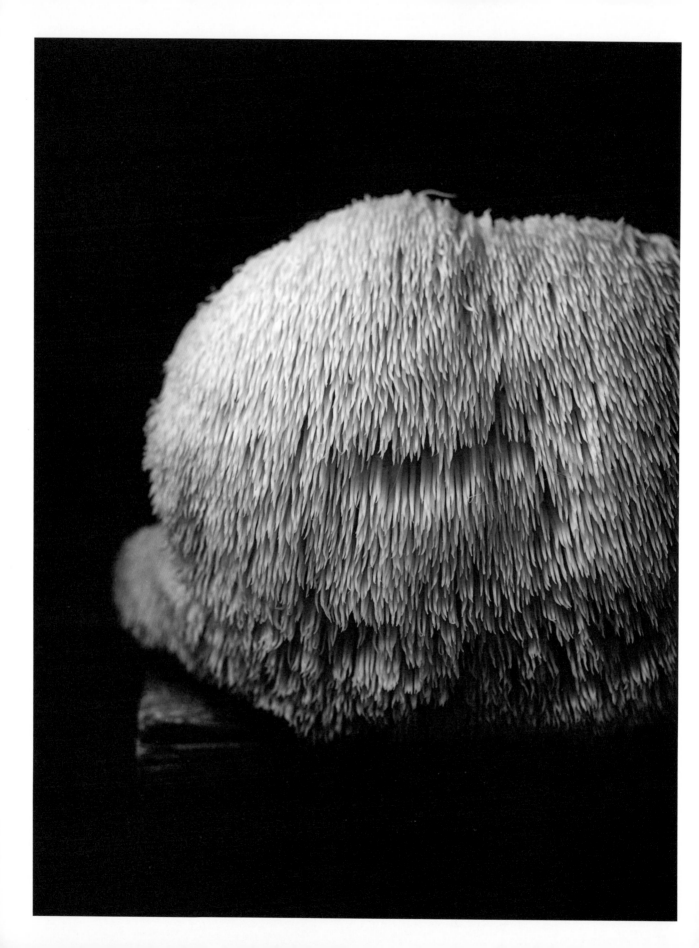

lion's mane mushroom mornay

SERVES 6 TO 8

When I was a child, my next-door neighbor, Miss Leslie, always had the most fabulous party on Christmas Eve. Upon entering her house there was a table full of the most delicious collection of dishes brought by all the guests. One of the most popular dishes at the party was my mother's crab dip: a creamy, cheesy sauce with jumbo lump crab meat. It was always one of the first dips to go, leaving the sad and hardly touched seven-layer dip feeling all kinds of resentment. Fast forward to when I moved back to Mississippi and went foraging one cold day in November. I stumbled upon some wild lion's mane mushrooms growing on the Natchez Trace Parkway. The first thing that popped into my head was the crab dip! You see, the texture of the lion's mane mushroom is succulent and delicately fibrous, just like crab meat. It's the *perfect* substitution. If you can't forage your own lion's mane or source any at your local farmers' market, you can easily substitute oyster, button, or shiitake mushrooms, although the texture won't be quite as spot on. The white wine and sherry provide the perfect roundness, just like the classic recipe. Note: This dip is indulgent and is meant for a party. Don't cut your eyes at me when you're reading the ingredient list!

2 cups filtered water

1 cup raw cashews

½ cup nutritional yeast

1 tablespoon mellow white miso or chickpea miso

1 tablespoon fresh lemon juice

1 pound lion's mane or white button mushrooms

½ cup vegan butter

½ cup minced shallots

3 garlic cloves, minced

2 tablespoons all-purpose flour

½ cup dry white wine

2 tablespoons sherry

Sea salt and freshly cracked black pepper

Thinly sliced green onions, for garnish

Fresh parsley, for garnish

Crackers, to dip

1. In a blender, combine the water, cashews, nutritional yeast, miso, and lemon juice and blend until smooth and creamy. Set the cashew cream aside.

2. If using lion's mane, tear into bite-size pieces. If using button, slice into bite-size pieces.

3. In a large skillet, heat the butter over medium heat. Add the shallots and garlic and cook, stirring frequently, until tender, about 5 minutes. Add the flour and mushrooms and cook for another 5 minutes. Add the white wine and sherry and use a wooden spatula to scrape the bottom of the pan. Cook for an additional 5 minutes. Reduce the heat to low and pour in the cashew cream, stirring frequently until the mixture becomes thick, similar to a dip. Season with salt and pepper to taste.

4. Transfer to a serving dish or small slow cooker and garnish with green onions and parsley. Serve with crackers.

CHAPTER 3

—

sandwiches
&
salads

lagniappe: *Depending on which brand of liquid smoke that you are using, you may be able to add more, which will give your bacon a smokier flavor. Just be careful, as some brands are stronger and more bitter than others.*

p.l.t.s

I created this recipe when I was in my early twenties and living in Charleston, South Carolina. I would invite my friends over and offer a buffet of toasted sourdough bread, a large pile of crispy iceberg lettuce, thick slices of juicy ripe tomatoes, a bucket of vegan mayo, and, the all-star ingredient, potato bacon. Now, I know what you're thinking . . . Potato bacon? Yes. Potato bacon. Didn't you know us vegans will make bacon out of practically anything? Well, except a pig! Thin slices of potato tossed with seasonings and baked until crispy and chewy make a fantastic alternative to traditional bacon. When you load up a sandwich piled high with all the fixings, you'll be hooked.

potato bacon

⅓ cup nutritional yeast, plus more for sprinkling

1 teaspoon smoked paprika

2 tablespoons maple syrup

1 teaspoon liquid smoke, plus more to taste

⅓ cup tamari or coconut aminos

¼ cup peanut oil

1 pound russet potatoes, rinsed and dried

Sea salt and freshly cracked black pepper

assembly

1 large sourdough round (or desired loaf of bread), sliced

Vegan mayo

1 head iceberg lettuce, leaves rinsed and separated

1 to 2 large heirloom tomatoes, rinsed and sliced

Avocado (optional)

1. Preheat the oven to 350°F. Line two large baking sheets with parchment paper.

2. **Make the potato bacon:** In a bowl, mix together the nutritional yeast, smoked paprika, maple syrup, liquid smoke, tamari, and peanut oil to create a marinade. Using a mandoline or a very sharp knife, carefully slice the potatoes lengthwise into thin, oval-shaped slices (about ¹⁄₁₆ inch thick). Toss in the marinade and let sit for about 15 minutes until the potatoes are soft and pliable.

3. Arrange the potato slices close together on the baking sheets. Using your fingers, squeeze and crinkle the slices, replicating the shape of cooked bacon. Drizzle the remaining marinade on top, sprinkle with a little nutritional yeast, and bake for 30 minutes. Remove from the oven and carefully flip the slices. Squeeze the potatoes again, to encourage crinkling, and sprinkle with salt and pepper to taste. Place the bottom baking sheet on the top rack, and vice versa, to promote even cooking. Bake the potatoes until crispy, yet slightly chewy . . . like bacon, another 20 minutes.

4. To assemble the sandwiches, toast the bread slices, spread on the vegan mayo, and add the lettuce, tomatoes, potato bacon, and avocado, if using. Serve.

grilled avocado kimchi sandwich

with garlic chive aioli

MAKES 2 SANDWICHES

I call this sandwich a grown-up vegan grilled cheese. Combining salty, tangy kimchi with creamy rich avocado and a garlicky aioli creates a powerhouse of flavor that is similar to cheese. If you've never had kimchi before, this is a great way to start, as it's not particularly overwhelming in this sandwich. The trick to this recipe is using really good bread and pan-frying till golden brown and crispy.

garlic chive aioli

1½ tablespoons olive oil

¼ to ½ cup chopped garlic, to taste

1 cup vegan mayo

¼ cup finely chopped garlic chives or regular chives

1 tablespoon fresh lemon juice

1 tablespoon nutritional yeast

½ teaspoon onion powder

½ teaspoon garlic powder

sandwich

4 slices bread of choice

4 teaspoons vegan butter or olive oil

1 small avocado

2 tablespoons Garlic Chive Aioli

¼ cup paper-thin slices red onion (optional)

¼ cup drained, packed Sunshine Kimchi (page 258) or store-bought vegan kimchi

1. In a skillet, heat the oil over medium heat. Add the garlic and cook, stirring constantly to prevent burning, until softened and caramelized. Transfer to a small bowl and stir in the mayo, chives, lemon juice, nutritional yeast, onion powder, and garlic powder. Mix well and set aside. This will make more than you need for the sandwiches; leftover aioli will keep in the fridge for a couple of days.

2. Spread some butter on each slice of bread. In a skillet over medium heat, grill the bread butter-side down, gently pressing on the slices with a spatula to ensure even browning. Remove the bread from the pan and get ready to assemble the sandwiches.

3. Halve and pit the avocado. Mash the avocado onto the untoasted sides of 2 slices of bread. These two pieces will be the base of your sandwich.

4. Spread 1 tablespoon of aioli on the other 2 slices. Top with onion, if using.

5. Lastly, distribute a thin layer of kimchi on top of the avocado slices. Place the slices with aioli onto the avocado slices and cut the sandwiches on a diagonal. Done!

fried popcorn tofu po' boys

MAKES 2 SANDWICHES

A po' boy, which literally means poor boy, is a traditional New Orleans sandwich. Crusty, flaky bread is scored down the middle and loaded with some sort of battered and fried protein, usually shrimp. Since their creation, they've become popular along the Gulf Coast and bordering Southern states. Today, they are even making their way onto menus across the rest of America. A "dressed" po' boy means you serve it with shredded lettuce, tomatoes, pickles, and mayo. Other popular condiments are ketchup, hot sauce, and Rémoulade (page 261). You can use whatever vegan protein you like for this recipe, but for this go-'round, I've included my popcorn tofu recipe. The Old Bay seasoning provides an uncanny "seafood" or "shrimp" flavor, while pan-frying then roasting the tofu gives it a chewy, meaty texture. This sandwich is a total mess to eat but that's part of the fun!

popcorn tofu

¼ cup corn flour

2 tablespoons Old Bay seasoning, plus more for sprinkling

2 tablespoons nutritional yeast

1 tablespoon cornstarch

Freshly cracked black pepper

1 block tofu, drained, patted dry, and cut into bite-size cubes

½ cup vegetable oil

fully dressed toppings

Two 8-inch po' boy baguettes, cut in half lengthwise

Vegan mayo

½ head thinly shredded iceberg lettuce

8 to 10 hamburger pickle slices

1 to 2 tomatoes, sliced

Ketchup

1. Preheat the oven to 350°F.

2. **Make the popcorn tofu:** In a shallow bowl, mix together the corn flour, Old Bay, nutritional yeast, cornstarch, and black pepper to taste. Add the tofu to the dredging mixture and toss, coating the pieces thoroughly.

3. In a large skillet, heat the oil over medium heat. When a sprinkling of batter sizzles, it's ready. Add the tofu and fry for a few minutes on each side, until golden brown and crispy all around. Once done, transfer the tofu to a baking sheet and bake for about 20 minutes, until the tofu becomes slightly more firm and springy in texture. At the very end, since the oven is already hot, pop the po' boy bread in to lightly toast.

3. To assemble the po' boys, spread the mayo on each side of the bread. Add the lettuce, pickles, tomatoes, and tofu. Drizzle on some ketchup, if desired, or serve on the side to dip.

lagniappe: *If you are having trouble finding traditional po' boy bread, try heading to a nearby Vietnamese restaurant. The bread used for a banh mi is exactly what you are looking for. If you ask nicely, I'm sure they would be happy to sell you a loaf or two. They always do when I inquire, but I'm also super adorable . . .*

avocado, cucumber & tomato salad

with zesty shallot garlic vinaigrette

SERVES 6 TO 8

This salad is dedicated to my father, as it has all of his favorite ingredients: avocado, cucumber, and juicy, ripe tomatoes. Honestly, these three ingredients are sublime on their own, with maybe just a sprinkling of sea salt. But for this recipe, I've created a well-rounded vinaigrette that's tangy and zesty. The secret ingredient is the white wine vinegar, which provides a subtle sweetness. Cooking the garlic and shallots in olive oil infuses their flavor throughout the oil used for the dressing, while a touch of raw garlic at the end adds that perfect zing. Sourcing perfectly ripe avocados and tomatoes is key for this salad. If they are not ripe enough, it can be a total deal breaker. So do me proud, please.

---

vinaigrette

½ cup extra virgin olive oil

1 cup minced shallots

¼ cup minced garlic + 1 to 2 teaspoons finely minced garlic

2 tablespoons fresh lemon juice

2 tablespoons white wine vinegar

2 teaspoons tamari

1 teaspoon Dijon mustard

1 teaspoon freshly cracked black pepper

½ teaspoon sea salt

½ teaspoon crushed red pepper flakes

½ teaspoon sugar

salad

1 cup cherry tomatoes (large ones halved, small ones left whole)

1 cup diced heirloom tomato

2 cups peeled and sliced cucumbers

1½ cups avocado chunks (about 1 large or 2 small avocados)

Chopped fresh chives, for garnish

1. **Make the vinaigrette:** In a large skillet, heat the olive oil over medium heat. Add the shallots and ¼ cup of garlic and sauté until they barely begin to brown. Remove from the heat and let cool. Scrape them out of the pan and into a large bowl. Add the lemon juice, vinegar, tamari, finely minced garlic, mustard, black pepper, salt, pepper flakes, and sugar. Mix well.

2. **Assemble the salad:** Gently fold the tomatoes, cucumbers, and avocado into the vinaigrette until everything is well coated. Garnish with chives and serve immediately.

lagniappe: *For this recipe, Sun Gold cherry tomatoes are my favorite to use, as they are incredibly sweet and juicy. If you are using English cucumbers, you can leave the skin on, as it is thin and crunchy. If you are using a traditional cucumber, I recommend peeling the skin off, since the waxy texture is not desirable. But that's up to you.*

avocado kale salad

SERVES 4

Simplicity at its best. Once massaged, the kale becomes tender and succulent, much like myself after a massage. With just a touch of garlic, ripe avocado, and a sprinkling of nutritional yeast, salt, and pepper, this is my go-to salad. Serve with rice, on toast, as a side, or in a wrap—you really can't go wrong here.

---

8 cups shredded kale
(about 6 ounces)

1 large ripe avocado, pitted
and scooped

1 garlic clove, finely minced
(use a garlic press or
Microplane)

2 tablespoons fresh lemon juice,
plus more for serving

2 tablespoons nutritional yeast,
plus more for serving

½ teaspoon freshly cracked
black pepper, or to taste

½ teaspoon sea salt, or to taste

In a large bowl, combine all of the ingredients. Using your hands, massage everything together for a few minutes, squeezing the kale as hard as you can. Once soft and tender, transfer to serving bowls. Garnish with a sprinkling of nutritional yeast and a spritz of lemon juice.

lagniappe: *This salad is* perfect *for making avocado toast. Garnish with cherry tomatoes, sliced radishes, cooked chickpeas, or whatever your heart desires. A sprinkling of smoked paprika never hurt nobody.*

roasted roots & quinoa salad

with meyer lemon miso-tahini dressing

SERVES 4 TO 6

Now, you girls and boys knew I couldn't write a vegan cookbook without including a hippie dippie, healthy salad with loads of quinoa, kale, and a miso-tahini dressing? No way! I simply had to. I mean, I have to pay tribute to what paved the way. Luckily, even though this salad showcases all of the classic, healthy vegan go-to's, it's loaded with flavor. You can use whatever root vegetables you desire, but I personally recommend radishes, rutabagas, turnips, carrots, and sweet potatoes. Once roasted, the sweetness from these roots pairs beautifully with the tangy, creamy dressing. I love using Meyer lemon juice because of its earthy sweetness. The quinoa provides that substantial amount of protein that vegans are just desperate for . . . that was a joke. Make the salad.

½ pound radishes, rinsed and cut into bite-size chunks

½ pound rutabaga, rinsed, peeled, and cut into bite-size chunks

4 shallots (about 5 ounces), peeled and halved

2 tablespoons vegetable oil

Sea salt and freshly cracked black pepper

1 tablespoon nutritional yeast (optional)

1 cup white quinoa

1 cup red or black quinoa

4 cups filtered water

3 cups packed chopped kale (about 3 ounces)

Two 5-ounce packages spring mix lettuce

Meyer Lemon Miso-Tahini Dressing (recipe follows)

Avocado slices, for serving (optional)

1. Preheat the oven to 450°F.

2. Toss the radishes, rutabaga, and shallots with the vegetable oil, ¼ teaspoon of sea salt, ¼ teaspoon of black pepper, and nutritional yeast, if using, on a parchment-lined baking sheet or in a large cast-iron skillet. Place in the oven and roast for 45 minutes, tossing halfway through. It's okay if the shallots fall apart while tossing.

3. In a large pot, combine the quinoa and water and bring to a boil. Once it boils, reduce the heat to a simmer and cook until done, 15 to 20 minutes. (If using a rice cooker, add the quinoa and water and cook.) Once the quinoa is done, mix in the kale, allowing the hot quinoa to wilt the greens. Season with salt and pepper to taste.

4. Transfer the quinoa and kale mixture, spring mix, and roasted vegetables to a large bowl and toss with a light drizzling of dressing.

5. Divide the mixture among individual serving bowls or place in one large serving bowl. Drizzle on the desired amount of dressing and serve. Top with avocado, if desired.

lagniappe: *This salad is delicious served warm or cold. Try packing some up for a picnic (with a bottle of wine).*

meyer lemon miso-tahini dressing

MAKES ¾ CUP

3 tablespoons tahini

3 tablespoons mellow white miso

2 tablespoons filtered water

2 tablespoons Meyer lemon juice

2 teaspoons toasted sesame oil

1 teaspoon maple syrup or agave

1 teaspoon nutritional yeast

1 teaspoon rice vinegar

Miso and tahini were meant to be together. They just were. Like, I don't make the rules here, people. For this dressing, I thinned out the dynamic duo with some fresh lemon juice, rice vinegar, and buttery toasted sesame oil, which echoes the flavor of the tahini paste. To make this recipe even more vegan than it already is, I added some nutritional yeast. Isa Chandra, this one's for you.

In a bowl, whisk together the tahini, miso, water, lemon juice, oil, maple syrup, nutritional yeast, and vinegar until smooth. Store in a tightly sealed container in the fridge for up to 1 week.

cucumber carrot salad

with umami dressing

SERVES 2 TO 4

This is one of my absolute favorite salads to make in the summer when local cucumbers are abundant and I want something light and refreshing. The dressing is the perfect example of umami. Ume plum vinegar with a splash of tamari and a sprinkling of nutritional yeast is a true powerhouse combination that coats your mouth with pure savory happiness. The perfect vehicle for this umami-packed dressing are crispy, delicate noodles of cucumber and sweet, crunchy carrots. You can simply stop there or add a sprinkling of gomashio and fresh herbs if you're looking for even more flavor.

umami dressing

1 tablespoon fresh lemon juice

2 teaspoons ume plum vinegar

1½ teaspoons tamari, or more to taste

2 tablespoons nutritional yeast

1 tablespoon toasted sesame oil

1 tablespoon olive oil

Freshly cracked black pepper

salad

3 cups julienned English cucumber (2 large)

2 cups julienned, peeled carrots (about 2 medium)

½ cup chopped fresh Thai basil or cilantro (optional)

½ cup thinly sliced radishes (optional)

Toasted Gomashio (page 268) or toasted peanuts (optional)

1. **Make the dressing:** In a large serving bowl, whisk together the lemon juice, vinegar, tamari, nutritional yeast, sesame oil, and black pepper to taste.

2. **Make the salad:** Place the cucumbers and carrot noodles on top of the dressing. If making ahead, keep covered in the fridge until ready to serve.

3. When ready to serve, toss the noodles with the dressing and eat as is or garnish with fresh herbs, radishes, and *gomashio*. Serve immediately. Note that the noodles will quickly become soggy, so don't dillydally!

lagniappe: *The easiest way to prepare the vegetables is by using a handheld julienne peeler, which is much safer than using a mandoline. Of course, a sharp knife will do as well.*

fig, beet & arugula salad

with creamy maple mustard dressing

SERVES 2 TO 4

Figs and the South simply go hand in hand—there are fig trees everywhere. Growing up, I remember harvesting them from a tree in my art teacher's backyard. I'd tear them open and squeeze their gooey, jamlike sweet filling straight into my mouth. It was like heaven. During a recent summer, my good friend Megan Elizabeth (who happens to be holding the salad in the picture to your left) was visiting. Being the fellow fig-fiend that she is, we were constantly eating them during her visit. Eventually, we asked ourselves, "What's a fun recipe we could make with figs?" She suggested that we make a creamy, sweet and savory dressing with toasted almond butter, maple syrup, and mustard . . . I suggested we use peppery arugula and earthy, succulent beets to contrast the figs' sweetness and crunch. Presto! This salad was born.

creamy maple mustard dressing

½ cup smooth almond butter

½ cup filtered water

3 tablespoons whole-grain or Dijon mustard

2 tablespoons maple syrup

2 teaspoons tamari

Dash cayenne pepper

salad

1 pound fresh figs, washed, stemmed, and quartered or halved, depending on size

2 medium beets, peeled, boiled, and cut into bite-size pieces (about 7 ounces)

5 ounces rinsed baby arugula

1. **Make the dressing:** In a large serving bowl, whisk together the almond butter, water, mustard, maple syrup, tamari, and cayenne until smooth.

2. **Assemble the salad:** Place the figs, beets, and arugula in the serving bowl on top of the dressing. If making ahead, cover and set in the fridge. When ready to serve, gently toss to coat with dressing and serve.

3. If you prefer less dressing, drizzle the desired amount on top of the salad and reserve any remaining dressing in a tightly sealed jar for up to 1 week.

lagniappe: *You might want to consider doubling the dressing recipe because it is good on everything! Try drizzling this dressing over roasted cauliflower or as a dip with celery and carrot sticks for a snack.*

vegan caesar

with creamy garlic dressing and fried capers

SERVES 4

This is my spin on a classic Caesar . . . The dressing is creamy, with just a touch of kala namak to replace the sulfury egg yolks used in the traditional dressing. Delicately seasoned croutons provide a nice crunch, while the crispy fried capers truly make this salad sing. If you've never had fried capers, you're welcome.

creamy garlic dressing

4 heads garlic

¼ cup olive oil, plus more for drizzling

3 tablespoons filtered water

2 tablespoons vegetable oil

2 teaspoons rice vinegar

2 teaspoons nutritional yeast

1 teaspoon stone-ground mustard

½ teaspoon kala namak salt

½ teaspoon vegan Worcestershire sauce

¼ teaspoon sugar

¼ teaspoon sea salt

¼ teaspoon freshly cracked black pepper

salad

3 cups cubed bread

2 tablespoons olive oil

1 tablespoon nutritional yeast

½ teaspoon onion powder

½ teaspoon garlic powder

¼ teaspoon freshly cracked black pepper

3 tablespoons vegetable oil

¼ cup capers, drained and dried

10 ounces chopped romaine lettuce

1. Preheat the oven to 350°F.

2. **Make the dressing:** Cut just the tops off the garlic heads so that you can squeeze out the cloves once they are roasted. Place them on a baking sheet and drizzle with olive oil. Bake until the tops of the cloves are golden brown and soft, 40 to 50 minutes, depending on the size of the garlic heads. Once cooled, you should be able to squeeze the cloves out easily. If not, pop them back in the oven until softer. Leave the oven on.

3. Squeeze the roasted garlic cloves into a small blender or food processor. Add the ¼ cup of olive oil, the water, vegetable oil, vinegar, nutritional yeast, mustard, kala namak, Worcestershire sauce, sugar, sea salt, and black pepper and blend until smooth.

4. **Make the salad:** In a bowl, toss the cubed bread with the olive oil, nutritional yeast, onion powder, garlic powder, and pepper. Mix well. Transfer to a baking sheet and bake until golden brown, about 25 minutes. Set the croutons aside.

5. In a sauté pan, heat the vegetable oil over medium heat. Add the capers and cook, stirring frequently, until they are crispy, 7 to 9 minutes. Drain them on a paper towel and set aside.

6. To assemble, add the greens to a large bowl. Drizzle on some Caesar dressing and toss to coat the greens with your desired amount of dressing and garnish with the capers and croutons.

pan-fried artichoke heart salad

with crushed castelvetrano olives

SERVES 4 TO 6

Artichokes were always on the table when I was growing up. Whole, stuffed artichokes at parties or artichoke hearts dipped in butter as a special treat—my family has always adored them. This dish is inspired by one of my favorite ingredients and a salad I once had at a small Italian restaurant in Brooklyn. I knew after the first bite that it would stick with me, so I re-created it so I could enjoy it at home. The combination of pan-fried artichoke hearts, salty olives, loads of caramelized onions, and a mountain of crispy browned garlic is out of this world. Try it out and let me know what you think. I'm dying to know.

One 7.5-ounce jar whole Castelvetrano olives, drained

2 tablespoons vegetable oil

1 pound drained whole artichoke hearts (one 33.5-ounce jar or 4 to 5 cans)

¼ cup roughly chopped garlic

1 heaping cup julienned red onions (about ½ large)

1 tablespoon fresh lemon juice, plus slices for garnish

Cold-pressed olive oil, for drizzling

Sea salt and freshly cracked black pepper

¼ cup chopped fresh oregano leaves

¼ cup chopped fresh parsley leaves

1. Using the flat side of a large knife, lightly press down on the olives, crushing them to reveal the pit. Discard the pits and set the olives aside.

2. In a large skillet, heat the oil over medium-high heat. Add the artichoke hearts and sear them for 12 minutes, flipping halfway through. The main goal here is to create some golden caramelization, so try not to stir them too much. If they do fall apart a bit, that's okay. Once they are browned, reduce the heat to medium.

3. Add the garlic and onions. Mix well and cook until they are tender and the garlic is slightly golden brown, about 5 minutes. Fold in the crushed olives and remove from the heat.

4. Transfer the mixture to a large salad bowl or serving platter. Drizzle with the lemon juice and some olive oil. Season with salt and pepper. Garnish with oregano and parsley leaves and lemon slices. Serve.

lagniappe: *Castelvetrano olives are my personal favorite because of their firm texture, buttery flavor, and bright green color. If you cannot find them, you can substitute good green olives instead. You can use whatever artichoke hearts you can find, but I prefer the whole baby ones packed in water because they are the most tender.*

picnic pasta salad

with oregano dill dressing

SERVES 6 TO 8

Pasta salad has always been one of my favorite picnic meals because it's delicious, portable, and easy to serve. Plus the bow-tie noodles are totally cute. It also happens to be one of my favorite ways to use fresh dill and oregano straight from the garden. The robust punch of these herbs blended with a creamy base really carries the dressing all the way to flavor town, while the parcooked vegetables provide the perfect amount of crunch. Throw in super ripe cherry tomatoes to give the salad a juicy sweetness and beautiful pop of color. It's the perfect crowd pleaser to bring to any party or picnic.

---

oregano dill dressing

1½ cups vegan mayo

½ cup finely chopped fresh oregano

½ cup finely chopped fresh dill

3 tablespoons fresh lemon juice

2 tablespoons white wine vinegar

2 tablespoons nutritional yeast

1 garlic clove, minced (use a garlic press or Microplane)

½ teaspoon sugar

½ teaspoon sea salt, or to taste

½ teaspoon freshly cracked black pepper, or to taste

Dash cayenne pepper

salad

1 pound bow-tie or squiggly pasta

3 cups bite-size pieces Broccolini (about 1 bunch)

2 cups bite-size pieces peeled carrots

½ cup frozen peas

1. **Make the dressing:** In a bowl, whisk together the mayo, oregano, dill, lemon juice, vinegar, nutritional yeast, garlic, sugar, sea salt, black pepper, and cayenne.

2. **Make the salad:** Fill a large bowl with ice and a little water to make an ice bath. This is to shock the vegetables, locking in their color and retaining their crunch, while also cooling down the pasta for the dressing.

3. Bring a large pot of salted water to a boil. Add the pasta and cook for about 7 minutes. Try a piece. When it feels close to being done, needing about 1 more minute, toss in the Broccolini, carrots, and peas. Cook for 1 to 2 more minutes, until the pasta is done. Drain and transfer to the ice bath.

recipe and ingredients continue

recipe continued from previous page

1 small red bell pepper, chopped

1 large cucumber, peeled and chopped

½ cup diced red onion

2 cups cherry or grape tomatoes, halved

½ cup high-quality pitted green olives, sliced

Sea salt and freshly cracked black pepper

Chopped fresh oregano and dill, for garnish

4. Once cooled, transfer the pasta/vegetables back to the colander and drain thoroughly. Excess water will dilute the dressing, which is a no-go, people.

5. In a large bowl, toss together the dressing, drained pasta/vegetable mixture, bell pepper, cucumber, red onion, tomatoes, and olives. Mix well. Season with sea salt and black pepper to taste. Garnish with the fresh dill and oregano. Serve.

lagniappe: *You can make this pasta salad the day before (or even two days before), as it keeps well in the fridge. Some might say it's even better the next day. For serving at a picnic, try using Chinese-food takeout containers and chopsticks.*

vegan chicken salad

with grapes & toasted pecans

SERVES 6 TO 8

My mama is known for her chicken salad, which features juicy, sweet red grapes and toasted pecans. When I was working on this recipe, she reminded me that her secret ingredient is curry powder. More of a secret weapon if you ask me! Earthy, spicy, and robust—a little goes a long way. But that little touch provides a beautiful depth of flavor. Green apple and celery give this salad a crispy crunch. Feel free to push and pull the seasonings with this recipe. For a fun variation, try adding a few teaspoons of grated fresh ginger and swapping out the grapes for raisins. I love munching on this salad with crackers at a picnic, but it works beautifully in a wrap or on toasted bread for a decadent sandwich.

1½ cups vegan mayo

2 tablespoons nutritional yeast

1 to 2 teaspoons curry powder, to taste

½ tablespoon fresh lemon juice

1 teaspoon garlic powder

1 teaspoon onion powder

1 garlic clove, minced (use a garlic press or Microplane)

2 cups chopped celery (4 to 5 stalks)

1½ cups halved red grapes (12 ounces)

1 cup diced Granny Smith apple (1 small)

1 cup chopped toasted pecans

1½ pounds vegan chicken-style strips, cooked and shredded

Sea salt and freshly cracked black pepper

Dash cayenne pepper (optional)

½ cup chopped green onions

1. In a large bowl, whisk together the mayo, nutritional yeast, curry powder, lemon juice, garlic powder, onion powder, and minced garlic.

2. Add the celery, grapes, apple, pecans, and shredded chicken. Mix well. Season with salt and black pepper to taste. Add the cayenne, if using. Garnish with the green onions. You're done! Serve with crackers, toast, or in a wrap.

lagniappe: *You can find vegan chicken-style "strips" or "breasts" in the refrigerated vegetarian meat section or the frozen section of most grocery stores. Avoid the kind with breading and feel free to substitute plain seitan, if you'd prefer. I recommend going with your favorite brand, one that you are comfortable with. For recommendations on my favorite brands, hop on over to my website.*

potato salad

with creamy creole dressing

SERVES 4 TO 6

Potato salad is a popular dish around the globe, with many different variations and dressings. But down here in the South, we like our potatoes *peeled* and tossed with a dressing that's *heavy* on the mayo! Every Southern family has their own variation, and this one is mine. And when it comes to this salad . . . I just can't. I can't handle how good it is. And by that, I mean that I actually could eat the whole bowl of it in front of you. But I'm not going to do that today. Instead, I'm just going to let you know that this creamy Creole dressing is popping off with flavor and herbs that beautifully coat tender chunks of perfectly cooked potatoes. The trick here is to boil the potato pieces in water flavored with sea salt, sugar, and vinegar. This is what we call *next level*. To push this salad way over the top, add a hefty sprinkling of shiitake bacon. Once you take a bite, you'll say the very same thing that I do, "I just can't."

potatoes

8 cups peeled and cubed (1-inch) russet potatoes (about 2 pounds)

1½ tablespoons sea salt

2 tablespoons sugar

2 tablespoons rice vinegar

1 tablespoon olive oil

creamy creole dressing

1 cup vegan mayo

3 tablespoons Dijon mustard

3 tablespoons fresh lemon juice

3 tablespoons nutritional yeast

1 garlic clove, finely minced

2 teaspoons tamari or coconut aminos

1 teaspoon sugar

½ teaspoon freshly cracked black pepper

½ teaspoon crushed red pepper flakes

1. **Prepare the potatoes:** Fill a large pot with water. Add the potatoes, salt, sugar, and vinegar to the pot, cover, and bring to a boil. Boil until the potatoes are firm-tender, about 20 minutes. You want them to keep their shape, so don't overcook them. Drain the potatoes in a colander and run cold water over them. Toss them in a serving bowl with the olive oil. Cover loosely and place in the fridge to cool thoroughly. If the potatoes are not completely cool, the dressing will break and become oily. No, ma'am!

2. **Make the dressing:** In a bowl, whisk together the mayo, mustard, lemon juice, nutritional yeast, garlic, tamari, sugar, black pepper, pepper flakes, cayenne, paprika, and sea salt to taste. Set aside.

¼ teaspoon cayenne pepper

¼ teaspoon sweet paprika

Sea salt

salad

½ cup chopped celery

¼ cup diced carrots,
  plus more for garnish

¼ cup diced red onion,
  plus more for garnish

3 tablespoons thinly sliced green
  onion, plus more for garnish

Chopped fresh parsley,
  for garnish (optional)

Shiitake Bacon (page 254)

3. Once the potatoes have cooled, add the celery, carrots, red onion, green onion, and desired amount of dressing (I use it all!). Gently fold everything together. Garnish with a sprinkling of the diced carrots and red onions, sliced green onions, and chopped parsley. Lastly, add as much shiitake bacon as you can fit on top and serve.

CHAPTER 4

–

soups
&
stews

sweet onion soup

SERVES 6 TO 8

This is French onion soup with a Southern nod. My tip is to always source young, fresh onions from the farmers' market, as they are much milder and sweet. If you are lucky enough to get your hands on some Vidalia onions, then you'd be just silly not to make this recipe. These unusually sweet onions are named after the city where they are grown: Vidalia, Georgia. And once you taste one, you'll understand what everyone is raving about. The shiitake mushroom stock in this recipe provides a buttery richness that pairs gorgeously with the tender, sweet strands of onions, while the wine and sherry provide that distinctive French onion soup flavor. Serve with crispy toasted bread and a light salad, and you've got yourself a fabulous meal.

---

mushroom stock

8 cups boiling water

12 ounces dried shiitake mushrooms

soup base

½ cup olive oil

3 pounds sweet onions, peeled, halved, and sliced

½ cup minced garlic

¼ cup nutritional yeast

1 tablespoon onion powder

1 tablespoon garlic powder

1 teaspoon dried thyme

4 cups filtered water

1 cup dry red wine

½ cup dry white wine

½ cup dry sherry

¼ cup tamari

2 tablespoons tomato paste

1 tablespoon rice vinegar

5 fresh bay leaves

Sea salt and freshly cracked black pepper

Chopped fresh chives, garlic chive flowers, or society garlic flowers, for garnish

1. **Make the mushroom stock:** Pour the boiling water over the dried shiitake mushrooms in a heatproof bowl. Let them soak for about 20 minutes, then strain the liquid through a fine-mesh sieve. Set aside. (You can reincorporate the rehydrated mushrooms into the soup if you'd like, simply chop them up and add them before bringing to a rapid boil.)

2. **Make the soup base:** In a large stockpot, heat the olive oil over medium-high heat. Add the onions and cook until they are soft and squishy, 10 to 15 minutes. Reduce the heat to medium and add the garlic. Cook, stirring frequently, until the onions are caramelized and dark in color, about 20 minutes.

3. Add the nutritional yeast, onion powder, garlic powder, and thyme and stir well. Cook for 5 minutes. Add the mushroom stock, the water, wines, sherry, tamari, tomato paste, vinegar, and bay leaves. Bring to a rapid boil and cook for 5 minutes. Reduce the heat to low and simmer for 20 minutes. Give it a taste and season with salt and pepper to your liking. When serving, discard the bay leaves and garnish with fresh herbs and flowers, if available.

hoppin' john stew

with okra & tomatoes

SERVES 8

Down here in the South, we are big on tradition. This stew is a tribute to that. Hoppin' John is a dish of seasoned black-eyed peas—which symbolize luck—and rice that we Southerners eat on New Year's Day to ring in the year ahead. It's typically served with cornbread, collard greens, and cabbage, which all represent wealth. For this spinoff, I use Hoppin' John as the base with the addition of okra, tomatoes, and vegetable stock. The result is an epic Southern stew that would be fantastic not only on New Year's Day but any day of the year.

½ cup olive oil

2 cups chopped onions

1 cup chopped celery

½ cup chopped red bell pepper

½ cup chopped green bell pepper

1 cup shredded cabbage

¼ cup finely chopped garlic

2 tablespoons nutritional yeast

1 teaspoon dried thyme

1 teaspoon onion powder

1 teaspoon garlic powder

1 teaspoon sugar

½ teaspoon smoked paprika

¼ teaspoon freshly grated nutmeg

½ teaspoon cayenne pepper (optional)

Freshly cracked black pepper

12 cups vegetable broth (preferably no salt added; and if so, be aware when seasoning)

1 pound dried black-eyed peas, rinsed and soaked overnight

One 14.5-ounce can fire-roasted diced tomatoes

1. In a large pot, heat the olive oil over medium heat. Add the onions and cook, stirring frequently, until soft and caramelized, about 10 minutes. Add the celery, bell peppers, cabbage, and garlic. Cook for another 10 minutes, stirring frequently so the garlic doesn't burn. Add the nutritional yeast, thyme, onion powder, garlic powder, sugar, smoked paprika, nutmeg, cayenne, if using, and ½ teaspoon of black pepper. Cook for another 5 minutes, stirring and mixing well, to toast all of the herbs and spices.

2. Add the vegetable broth, black-eyed peas, canned tomatoes, cherry tomatoes, vinegar, and liquid smoke. Mix well and bring to a boil. Boil the soup for a solid 5 minutes. Reduce the heat to low and cook, stirring occasionally, until the black-eyed peas are soft and tender, about 1 hour.

3. Once the peas are done, add the tamari, 2 teaspoons sea salt, the shredded greens, and okra. Cook until the greens are wilted and the okra is tender, an additional 10 to 15 minutes. Give it a taste and season with more salt and pepper as desired.

1 to 2 cups sliced cherry
  tomatoes, reserving some
  for garnish

1 tablespoon red wine vinegar

1 teaspoon liquid smoke

1 tablespoon tamari or
  coconut aminos

Sea salt

2 cups shredded kale or
  collard greens

1 to 2 cups fresh or frozen
  sliced okra, to taste

Toasted Louisiana Popcorn Rice
  (page 171) or Creole Rice
  (page 160), for serving

Thinly sliced green onions,
  for garnish

Chopped fresh parsley,
  for garnish

4. Ladle a few scoops of the stew into serving bowls and place a scoop of rice on top of each serving. Sprinkle with green onions, parsley, and the reserved cherry tomato slices. Enjoy!

lagniappe: *The black-eyed peas need to soak overnight in a covered bowl.*

succotash stew

SERVE 6 TO 8

Succotash is a Southern medley of lima beans, corn, and other mixed vegetables. This recipe transforms that simple side dish into a hearty vegetable stew. Loaded with shredded cabbage, carrots, green beans, and, of course, lima beans and corn, this soup is a total crowd pleaser. Garnish with fresh cherry tomatoes and a scoop of fluffy rice for a delightful supper.

½ cup olive oil

3 cups shredded cabbage (about ½ head)

1 large onion, chopped

2 cups chopped celery (about 3 large stalks)

1 cup corn kernels, fresh (about 2 ears) or frozen

1 cup chopped carrots

1 cup chopped (⅓-inch pieces) green beans

⅓ cup chopped garlic

1 tablespoon sea salt, or to taste

1 teaspoon freshly cracked black pepper, or to taste

1 teaspoon sugar

2 tablespoons dried thyme

2 tablespoons dried parsley

1 tablespoon dried oregano

1 teaspoon crushed red pepper flakes (optional)

3 tablespoons nutritional yeast

2 tablespoons onion powder

2 tablespoons garlic powder

1. In a large pot, heat the oil over medium heat. Throw in the cabbage, onion, and celery and cook, stirring frequently, until soft and caramelized, about 10 minutes.

2. Add the corn, carrots, green beans, and garlic and cook for another 10 minutes, stirring often to prevent the garlic from burning. Add the salt, black pepper, sugar, dried thyme, dried parsley, dried oregano, pepper flakes, if using, and nutritional yeast and mix well. Cook for another 5 minutes until fragrant.

3. In a small bowl, mix together the onion powder, garlic powder, tamari, vinegar, and tomato paste. Mix until well combined. Add this along with the broth, water, bay leaves, and lima beans. Mix well.

recipe and ingredients continue

recipe continued from previous page

3 tablespoons tamari or coconut aminos

3 tablespoons rice vinegar or apple cider vinegar

1 tablespoon tomato paste

6 cups vegetable broth

4 cups filtered water

6 large dried bay leaves

3 cups baby lima beans, fresh or frozen

1 tablespoon chopped fresh oregano

1 tablespoon chopped fresh parsley, plus more for garnish

2 tablespoons chopped fresh thyme leaves

2 cups halved cherry tomatoes

4. Bring to a boil and cook for 5 minutes. Reduce the heat to low and partially cover with a lid. Cook until the lima beans are tender, 20 to 30 minutes. Give it a taste and season with more salt and pepper if needed. Add the fresh oregano, parsley, thyme, and cherry tomatoes. Cook for a final 5 minutes. Discard the bay leaves. Serve garnished with fresh parsley to make it super pretty.

lagniappe: *If using fresh corn kernels, don't even think about tossing the cobs! They're loaded with flavor. Throw them in the stew once all of the liquid has been added. This will provide a buttery, rich flavor to the stock. When ready to serve, simply remove the cobs.*

mama's rosemary white bean soup

SERVES 4 TO 6

My mama always makes this soup when I come home to visit. She's very proud of how delicious it is, and, I must admit, I have to agree. Creamy white beans are the perfect blank canvas for an herb like rosemary. If you use too much, it can be a bit overwhelming, but this soup has *just* the right amount. One key ingredient is the carrots, which bring a subtle sweetness and a hint of color. Heads up! You will need to soak the beans for at least a couple of hours, so I recommend covering them with water in a bowl and leaving them on the counter overnight.

¼ cup olive oil

1 cup chopped celery (about 3 stalks, with tops)

½ cup chopped green bell pepper

½ cup chopped red bell pepper

2 cups chopped onion (about 1 large)

1 cup large chunks peeled carrots

2 or 3 fresh bay leaves or 4 dried

3 tablespoons chopped fresh rosemary, plus more for garnish

1 tablespoon diced garlic

2 teaspoons chopped fresh thyme

1 pound dried Great Northern beans, soaked overnight, rinsed, and drained

7 cups water or vegetable broth

1 teaspoon liquid smoke

1 teaspoon smoked sea salt

Splash tamari

4 green onions, thinly sliced, plus more for garnish

½ cup chopped fresh parsley, plus more for garnish

Sea salt and freshly cracked black pepper

Dash red pepper flakes (optional)

Cooked rice (optional)

1. In a heavy pot, heat the olive oil over medium-high heat. Add the trinity (celery, bell peppers, and onion). Cook until translucent. Add the carrots, bay leaves, rosemary, garlic, and thyme and cook for 5 minutes, stirring frequently, until it smells lovely.

2. Add the beans, water, liquid smoke, smoked sea salt, and tamari. Bring to a boil and cook for 5 minutes. Reduce the heat to low, cover, and cook for about 1 hour, stirring occasionally.

3. Once the soup has reduced and thickened, add 1 to 2 cups more water if desired for a thinner consistency. Continue cooking until the beans are soft and tender, about 2 hours of total cooking time. Add the green onions and parsley. Season with salt and black pepper to taste and add the pepper flakes, if desired. Mix well.

4. Discard the bay leaves. Serve with a scoop of white rice, if using. Garnish with additional green onions, parsley, and fresh rosemary.

mirliton corn bisque

SERVES 6 TO 8

Mirlitons, also known as chayotes, are odd-looking, pear-shaped green vegetables related to zucchini and squash. Because of their abundance in southern Louisiana, they've become a traditional ingredient in Cajun cooking. In this creamy corn bisque, the chunks of mirlitons absorb the buttery corn broth, becoming succulent and juicy. For a variation, try blending the soup for a silky-smooth and luxurious texture.

---

4 ears of corn

¼ cup olive oil

5 cups chopped peeled mirlitons (about 4)

1 large onion, chopped

1 cup chopped celery (3 to 4 stalks)

¾ cup chopped orange bell pepper (about 1 pepper)

¼ cup chopped garlic

7 cups filtered water

1 teaspoon rice vinegar

1½ teaspoons sea salt, or to taste

¼ teaspoon cayenne pepper, or to taste

½ cup raw cashews

Freshly cracked black pepper

Chopped fresh chives or green onion

1. Cut the corn kernels off the cobs and transfer to a large pot. Set the cobs aside.

2. Add the olive oil to the pot and heat over medium heat. Add the mirlitons, onion, celery, bell pepper, and garlic. Mix well. Once the vegetables are sizzling, reduce the heat to medium-low and cook, stirring frequently, until the vegetables are soft and tender, about 30 minutes. You want to avoid browning the vegetables so that the soup is a beautiful yellow, not brown. Reduce the heat if needed.

3. Once the vegetables have cooked down, add the corncobs, water, vinegar, sea salt, and cayenne. Bring to a boil and cook for 5 minutes. Reduce the heat to medium-low and simmer for another 20 minutes.

4. After 20 minutes, discard the corncobs and transfer 2 cups of the soup (with broth) to a blender along with the cashews. Blend on high until smooth and transfer back to the soup. Season with more salt and black pepper to taste.

5. Ladle the soup into serving bowls and garnish with freshly cracked black pepper and chives.

lagniappe: *If you can't find mirlitons at your local grocery store or farmers market, look for them at your local international market. Choose mirlitons that are bright green and firm to touch. The outer skin is thin and easy to peel. Once cut in half, simply remove the pit.*

oyster mushroom soup

SERVES 6 TO 8

I have a thing for nutrient-dense, brothy soups, especially when they are loaded with powerhouse ingredients like ginger, miso, lemongrass, bay leaves, and oyster mushrooms. Fun fact: Did you know that oyster mushrooms grow in the wild? I've happily harvested them multiple times here in Mississippi. Not only that, but they are also incredibly easy to grow *indoors*. There are many kits available on the market and let me tell you—it is so much fun to watch them grow. For example, hop on over to page 282 to check out a beautiful pink variety I grew in my very own kitchen. What a hoot!

⅓ cup olive oil

3 cups chopped leeks, white part only

1 cup chopped celery

¼ cup minced garlic

2 tablespoons minced or Microplaned fresh ginger

3 tablespoons mellow white miso or chickpea miso

1 tablespoon garlic powder

1 tablespoon onion powder

5 cups vegetable or mushroom broth

5 cups filtered water

3 cups oyster mushrooms, thickly sliced (about 4 ounces)

2 cups peeled and julienned carrot (about 1 large)

5 large dried bay leaves

1 stalk lemongrass, crushed with a rolling pin

2 tablespoons tamari or coconut aminos

1½ tablespoons fresh lemon juice

1 tablespoon rice vinegar

1-inch piece dried kombu

1 tablespoon sea salt, or to taste

½ teaspoon freshly cracked black pepper, or to taste

1. In a large pot, heat the olive oil over medium-high heat. Add the leeks and celery and sauté until translucent, about 10 minutes. Add the garlic and ginger. Cook for another 5 minutes. Add the miso, garlic powder, and onion powder and cook for another 5 minutes.

2. Add the vegetable broth, water, oyster mushrooms, carrots, bay leaves, lemongrass, tamari, lemon juice, vinegar, and kombu, if using. Mix well. Bring to a boil and cook for 5 minutes. Reduce the heat to low and cook for another 30 minutes. Season with the salt and pepper. Discard the bay leaves and kombu and serve.

peanut stew

with fresh greens

SERVES 6

Peanuts are big in the South. We just love 'em down here. They are widely cultivated and are therefore significantly consumed throughout the region. Boiled, fried, roasted, or ground into butter—we just can't get enough! But did you know that peanut butter also makes a fantastic base for soup? It creates a rich and creamy texture that is undeniably satisfying. This hearty stew has peanut butter, along with earthy cumin, fragrant coriander, and spicy curry powder. Throw in some fresh greens at the very last minute and serve with a scoop of piping-hot rice for a wholesome bowl of deliciousness.

¼ cup peanut oil

1 large onion, chopped

2 cups roughly chopped carrots (2 to 3 carrots)

¼ cup chopped garlic

2 inches fresh ginger, peeled and minced (or use a Microplane)

1 jalapeño pepper, seeded and minced (leave seeds if desired)

1 teaspoon ground coriander

1 teaspoon ground cumin

1 teaspoon dried thyme

½ teaspoon curry powder

¼ teaspoon ground turmeric

1 teaspoon sea salt, plus more to taste

½ cup natural unsweetened peanut butter (creamy or chunky)

2 tablespoons tomato paste

4 cups vegetable broth

1. In a large pot, heat the oil over medium heat. Throw in the onion and cook until translucent, about 10 minutes. Add the carrots, garlic, ginger, jalapeño, coriander, cumin, thyme, curry powder, turmeric, and salt. Stir and cook until the garlic is tender and the spices are fragrant, about 5 minutes.

2. Stir in the peanut butter and tomato paste. Add the broth, canned tomatoes, and bay leaves. Bring to a boil, then reduce the heat to medium-low and simmer, stirring occasionally, for about 20 minutes. Give it a taste and season with salt, if needed. Stir in the lime juice.

One 14.5-ounce can fire-roasted diced tomatoes

4 dried bay leaves

2 tablespoons fresh lime juice (about 2 limes)

1 to 2 bunches fresh greens (kale, spinach, or Swiss chard), rinsed and roughly torn

Basmati Cumin Rice (page 159) or desired grain

Chopped fresh cilantro, for garnish

Chopped salted roasted peanuts, for garnish

3. Before serving, throw in the greens. These will only take a minute or two to cook in the hot soup. Discard the bay leaves. Ladle the soup into bowls and garnish with the rice, cilantro, and chopped peanuts.

lagniappe: *If you have a peanut allergy or flat-out just don't like them, try using roasted almond butter instead. This will help create that creamy texture you're looking for.*

CHAPTER 5

—

gumbo,
rice &
mains

ONE OF MY FONDEST MEMORIES FROM CHILDHOOD IS waking up late on a weekend morning and smelling my mother cooking up the "trinity" for a large pot of gumbo. When the celery, green bell pepper, and onions (these three combined are the trinity) hit that piping-hot roux of oil and toasted flour, the most glorious smell would permeate the whole house. Once the trinity softened, she'd throw in the garlic, which made our tummies grumble with delight. As the gumbo continued to cook through the day, the whole house would smell outrageously delicious.

Lucky for me, gumbo was one of the very first things that I learned to cook. I remember it like it was yesterday: I was around fifteen years old and I asked my mother if she would teach me how to make this delicious, robust stew of a dish. Of course she agreed. Working through the process with her was extremely impactful for me as a young cook because it taught me how to layer ingredients and spices and build flavor to create a sophisticated and complex dish.

When it comes down to it, there are many different ways to make gumbo. The basic concept is that you brown flour with a fat, and then add a rich broth, along with okra and a variety of proteins, spices, and garnishes, to create a thick stew. Some cooks use ground sassafras leaves known as filé powder—which was introduced to the Cajuns by southern Native Americans—to thicken gumbo. Family gumbo recipes can be super thick, or they can be thinner (my father always preferred more roux and would make more to add to my mother's!). My family has always used tomatoes in their gumbo, which I quite like, so that's the way I do it. Crispy French bread smothered in butter is usually served on the side, though in some regions, a side of potato salad is more common. No matter what, freshly cooked rice, green onions, and parsley are a must.

Now, I know what you're thinking, "But how can you make gumbo *vegan*?" Well, that's simple. Let's not forget what this African word actually means: okra. In my humble opinion, that means okra (a *vegan* ingredient) in fact is the most important ingredient of all, one that should shine throughout the dish and be celebrated.

It's true that, traditionally, seafood, smoked ham, and sausage are used in most recipes. You could simply remove these ingredients and call it gumbo, but that's not what I do. Instead, I've created a powerful combination of spices and herbs to elevate the taste without the meat. The next few recipes are my favorite variations of this classic dish—all of which are as rich and satisfying as traditional gumbos. No one will miss a thing; they'll be too busy enjoying it for what it is: pure comfort in a bowl.

To cook the roux, I recommend using a large cast-iron skillet. (If you do not have one, you can use any large skillet.) To stir the roux, it's best to use a long-handled, flat-edged wooden spatula. There are specific ones that have a slight curve to them, which are called "roux spoons." I can't emphasize enough how much easier your life will be if you get one of these—not only will the length of the spoon protect your hands from scalding, but the long, flat edge will stir the mixture evenly and prevent it from burning. Remember, practice makes perfect. And if you burn a roux, you'll have to throw it out, as it will be too bitter. But that's okay. Anyone who makes gumbo has burned a roux at one point or another, although they might not admit it. It happens!

I know some folks have an aversion to the slimy texture of okra. If you're making gumbo for guests, you can try pan-frying the okra separately and using it as a garnish instead of incorporating into the stew. Of course, if you don't like okra at all, you can also take it out; just don't tell me about it.

With all of the vegetable prep you will be doing to make this dish, there will be plenty of scraps left over that are perfect for making any of the rice recipes on pages 159 to 165. If you'd like to try using filé powder, you can often find it in the spice section of the grocery store, or you can easily find it online. I make my own, as there is an abundance of sassafras trees throughout the Southeast.

classic gumbo

SERVES 6 TO 8

If you've never made gumbo before, this is a good place to start. Once you have perfected this foundational recipe, the sky is the limit when it comes to what you can do with it—you can add a savory protein such as my Barley Sausage (page 57) or Smoky Baked Tofu (page 164). For a lighter and more vegetable-focused version of this dish, try using shredded artichoke hearts, large chunks of carrots, squash, or zucchini.

2 cups chopped onion
(1 medium)

2 cups chopped celery
(about 4 large stalks)

1½ cups chopped green bell
pepper (about 1 large)

½ cup diced red bell pepper
(about 1 small)

½ cup minced garlic

8 cups vegetable broth

One 14.5-ounce can fire-roasted
diced tomatoes

1 cup diced fresh tomatoes

½ cup red wine

1 tablespoon tamari

1 tablespoon tomato paste

1 tablespoon ume plum vinegar

1 tablespoon vegan
Worcestershire sauce

2 tablespoons + ½ cup chopped
fresh parsley, plus more for
garnish

2 tablespoons chopped fresh
oregano

1 tablespoon chopped fresh
thyme

1 tablespoon minced jalapeño
pepper (optional)

1 teaspoon stone-ground
mustard or Creole mustard

1. In a bowl, combine the onion, celery, bell peppers, and garlic. Remove 1½ cups of this mixture and transfer to a separate bowl (you'll add this to the gumbo toward the end). Set both bowls aside.

2. In a large bowl, mix together the vegetable broth, canned tomatoes, fresh tomatoes, wine, tamari, tomato paste, vinegar, Worcestershire sauce, 2 tablespoons of the parsley, the oregano, thyme, jalapeño, if using, mustard, and liquid smoke. Set aside.

3. Now you are ready to make the roux! In a large clean, well-greased cast-iron skillet (be sure to wipe out any residue), heat the peanut oil over medium-high heat. Once it's hot, add the flour and stir constantly with a large wooden spatula, until it is well combined. Reduce the heat to medium and continue stirring until the roux is dark brown, 15 to 20 minutes. The goal here is to toast the flour and oil while preventing the mixture from burning. You do this by moving the flour and oil mixture constantly. If you stop for only a moment, the roux will burn and you will have to start over.

4. Reduce the heat to medium-low and add the larger amount of the onion mixture (not the reserved 1½ cups). Continue cooking, stirring constantly, until the vegetables are soft, 5 to 7 minutes.

recipe continues

recipe continued from previous page

1 teaspoon liquid smoke

1 cup peanut oil

1¼ cups all-purpose flour

Creole Spice Blend (page 250)

6 to 8 bay leaves, depending on size and desired amount

½ cup chopped green onions, plus more for garnish

2 to 3 cups chopped okra, or desired amount

Sea salt and freshly cracked black pepper

1 to 2 cups filtered water (optional)

3 to 4 cups cooked rice, for serving

5. Add the Creole spice blend and mix well. Cook for another 5 minutes, stirring frequently, toasting all of the spices. Now you have the base of your gumbo!

6. Transfer the base to a large stockpot. Add the broth mixture and bay leaves. Mix well and bring to a boil, stirring often to prevent the bottom from burning. Once at a boil, reduce the heat to low and simmer for 40 minutes, stirring occasionally, to reduce and thicken the gumbo.

7. Add the green onions, okra, the remaining ½ cup parsley, and the reserved 1½ cups onion mixture. If desired, add 1 to 2 cups water to loosen the gumbo. Simmer for another 20 minutes. Give the gumbo a taste and season with salt and pepper as needed. Feel free to add more cayenne pepper at this point to make it spicy as well.

8. To serve, ladle the gumbo into serving bowls, removing any bay leaves. Add a small scoop of cooked rice on top and garnish with the chopped parsley and green onions.

gumbo z'fungi

with sorghum-flour roux

SERVES 6 TO 8

This gumbo is for anyone who is gluten-free or prefers to avoid gluten whenever possible. After playing with many different gluten-free flours, I found that sorghum flour works best in re-creating a traditional roux, as it is mild and slightly sweet in flavor. The texture, of course, is not exactly like traditional gumbo, but it's pretty damn close! To help, I've paired this gluten-free roux with an umami-rich broth made from dried shiitakes. Once the shiitakes are rehydrated, they have a meaty, chewy texture. Add more chopped fresh mushrooms of any variety for a gumbo that is incredibly satisfying. As for dried mushrooms that have been cultivated indoors, they are usually clean when harvested. But just to be safe, I always strain their broth and give them a quick rinse after being hydrated.

8 cups boiling water

12 ounces dried shiitake mushrooms

1 pound fresh mushrooms (your choice), cleaned and roughly chopped

2 cups chopped onion (1 medium)

2 cups chopped celery (about 4 large stalks)

1½ cups chopped green bell pepper (about 1 large)

½ cup diced red bell pepper (about 1 small)

½ cup minced garlic

2 tablespoons + ½ cup chopped fresh parsley, plus more for garnish

2 tablespoons chopped fresh oregano

1 tablespoon chopped fresh thyme

One 14.5-ounce can fire-roasted diced tomatoes

1. Pour the boiling water over the dried shiitake mushrooms in a heatproof bowl. Let them soak for 20 to 30 minutes. Strain the liquid through a fine-mesh sieve. Set the liquid aside. Rinse the rehydrated mushrooms, removing any grit. Discard the stems and roughly chop the caps. Combine the shiitakes with the chopped fresh mushrooms in a bowl and set aside.

2. In a bowl, combine the onion, celery, bell peppers, and garlic. Remove 1½ cups of this mixture and transfer to a separate bowl (you'll add this to the gumbo toward the end). Set both bowls aside.

3. In a large bowl, combine the mushroom broth, 2 tablespoons of the parsley, the oregano, thyme, canned tomatoes, fresh tomatoes, tomato paste, mustard, tamari, Worcestershire sauce, liquid smoke, vinegar, wine, and jalapeños, if using. Mix until well combined.

4. Now you are ready to make the roux! In a large clean, well-greased cast-iron skillet (be sure to wipe out any residue), heat the peanut oil over medium-high heat. Once it's hot,

recipe and ingredients continue

recipe continued from previous page

1 cup diced fresh tomatoes

1 tablespoon tomato paste

1 teaspoon stone-ground
    mustard or Creole mustard

1 tablespoon tamari

1 tablespoon vegan
    Worcestershire sauce

1 teaspoon liquid smoke

1 tablespoon ume plum vinegar

½ cup red wine

1 tablespoon minced jalapeño
    pepper (optional)

¾ cup peanut oil

1 cup sweet white sorghum flour

Creole Spice Blend (page 250)

6 to 8 bay leaves, depending on
    size and desired amount

½ cup chopped green onions,
    plus more for garnish

2 to 3 cups chopped okra,
    or desired amount

1 to 2 cups filtered water

Sea salt and freshly cracked
    black pepper

3 to 4 cups cooked rice,
    for serving

Shiitake Bacon (page 254), for
    serving (optional)

add the sorghum flour and stir constantly with a large wooden spatula, until it is well combined. Reduce the heat to medium and continue stirring until the roux is dark brown, 15 to 20 minutes. The goal here is to toast the flour and oil while preventing the mixture from burning. You do this by moving the flour and oil mixture constantly. If you stop for only a moment, the roux will burn and you will have to start over.

5. Reduce the heat to medium-low and add the larger amount of the onion mixture (not the reserved 1½ cups). Continue cooking, stirring constantly, until the vegetables are soft, 5 to 7 minutes.

6. Add the Creole spice blend and mix well. Cook for another 5 to 7 minutes, stirring frequently. Now you have the base of your gumbo!

7. Transfer the base to a large stockpot. Add the broth mixture and the bay leaves. Mix well and bring to a boil, stirring often to prevent the bottom from burning. Cover and bring to a boil. Once at a boil, reduce the heat to low and simmer for 40 minutes, stirring occasionally, to reduce and thicken the gumbo.

8. Add the green onions, okra, remaining ½ cup parsley, and the reserved 1½ cups onion mixture. Simmer for another 20 minutes. If desired, add 1 to 2 cups water to loosen the gumbo. Give the gumbo a taste and season with salt and pepper. Feel free to add more cayenne pepper at this point to make it spicy as well.

9. To serve, ladle the gumbo into serving bowls, removing any bay leaves. Add a small scoop of cooked rice on top and garnish with chopped parsley, green onions, and a hefty sprinkling of shiitake bacon, if desired.

gumbo z'herbes

SERVES 6 TO 8

This is a traditional vegetarian version of gumbo created for Good Friday. Funny enough, most recipes I've seen still have plenty of meat added for flavoring . . . well, not in this cookbook! I use the same rich, plant-based base as I use in my other gumbo recipes, and add as many greens as I can fit in the pot. Feel free to use a variety of any leafy green vegetable. Usually they cook down quite a bit, so the best method is to add different varieties in increments. For an even fresher variation, simply pour the hot gumbo over chopped fresh greens like spinach or kale—they will cook right there in the bowl.

2 cups chopped onion
(1 medium)

2 cups chopped celery
(about 4 large stalks)

1½ cups chopped green bell
pepper (about 1 large)

½ cup diced red bell pepper
(about 1 small)

½ cup minced garlic

9 cups vegetable broth

2 tablespoons + ½ cup chopped
fresh parsley, plus more for
garnish

2 tablespoons chopped fresh
oregano

1 tablespoon chopped fresh
thyme

One 14.5-ounce can fire-roasted
diced tomatoes

1 cup diced fresh tomatoes

1 teaspoon stone-ground
mustard or Creole mustard

1 tablespoon tomato paste

1 tablespoon tamari

1 tablespoon vegan
Worcestershire sauce

1 teaspoon liquid smoke

1 tablespoon ume plum vinegar

1. In a bowl, combine the onion, celery, bell peppers, and garlic. Remove 1½ cups of this mixture and transfer to a separate bowl (you'll add this to the gumbo toward the end). Set both bowls aside.

2. In a large bowl, combine the vegetable broth, 2 tablespoons of the parsley, the oregano, thyme, canned tomatoes, fresh tomatoes, mustard, tomato paste, tamari, Worcestershire sauce, liquid smoke, vinegar, wine, and jalapeño, if using. Mix until well combined.

3. Now you are ready to make the roux! In a large clean, well-greased cast-iron skillet (be sure to wipe out any residue), heat the peanut oil over medium-high heat. Once it's hot, add the sorghum flour and stir constantly with a large wooden spatula until it is well combined. Reduce the heat to medium and continue stirring until the roux is dark brown, 15 to 20 minutes. The goal here is to toast the flour and oil while preventing the mixture from burning. You do this by moving the flour and oil mixture constantly. If you stop for only a moment, the roux will burn and you will have to start over.

4. Reduce the heat to medium-low and add the larger amount of the onion mixture (not the reserved 1½ cups). Continue cooking, stirring constantly, until the vegetables are soft, 5 to 7 minutes.

½ cup red wine

1 tablespoon minced jalapeño pepper (optional)

1 cup peanut oil

1¼ cups all-purpose flour

Creole Spice Blend (page 250)

6 to 8 bay leaves, depending on size and desired amount

½ cup chopped green onions, plus more for garnish

2 to 3 cups chopped okra, or desired amount

2 cups chopped kale

2 cups chopped collard greens

2 cups chopped Swiss chard or beet tops

1 to 2 cups chopped turnip greens

2 cups fresh spinach

1 to 2 cups filtered water (optional)

Sea salt and freshly cracked black pepper

3 to 4 cups cooked rice, for serving

5. Add the Creole spice blend and mix well. Cook for another 5 to 7 minutes, stirring frequently. Now you have the base of your gumbo!

6. Transfer the base to a large stockpot. Add the vegetable broth mixture and bay leaves. Mix well and bring to a boil, stirring often to prevent the bottom from sticking. Once at a boil, reduce the heat to low and simmer for 40 minutes, stirring occasionally, to reduce and thicken the gumbo.

7. Add the green onions, okra, kale, collards, Swiss chard, spinach, remaining ½ cup parsley, and the reserved 1½ cups onion mixture. Simmer for another 20 minutes. If desired, add 1 to 2 cups water to loosen the gumbo. Give the gumbo a taste and season with salt and pepper. Feel free to add more cayenne pepper at this point to give it some spice.

8. To serve, ladle the gumbo into serving bowls, removing any bay leaves. Add a small scoop of cooked rice on top and garnish with the chopped parsley and green onions.

lagniappe: *You might be wondering why you are adding the same ingredients at different stages throughout this recipe. Hop on over to page 41 to read about 2x to 3x ingredients to better understand why.*

gumbo z'maize

SERVES 6 TO 8

You should make this gumbo in the summer when juicy, sweet corn and young, tender okra are abundant. Cooking the gumbo with fresh corncobs creates a buttery, rich broth that's full of body and flavor. Topping the bowls with pan-fried corn kernels and tender okra is a festive and delightful way to celebrate the summer's bounty.

2 cups chopped onion (1 medium)

2 cups chopped celery (about 4 large stalks)

1½ cups chopped green bell pepper (about 1 large)

½ cup diced red bell pepper (about 1 small)

½ cup minced garlic

8 cups filtered water, plus 1 to 2 cups to loosen the gumbo (optional)

2 tablespoons + ½ cup chopped fresh parsley

2 tablespoons chopped fresh oregano

1 tablespoon chopped fresh thyme

One 14.5-ounce can fire-roasted diced tomatoes

1 cup diced fresh tomatoes

1 teaspoon stone-ground mustard or Creole mustard

1 tablespoon tomato paste

1 tablespoon tamari

1 tablespoon vegan Worcestershire sauce

1 teaspoon liquid smoke

1 tablespoon ume plum vinegar

½ cup red wine

1 tablespoon minced jalapeño pepper (optional)

1. In a bowl, combine the onion, celery, bell peppers, and garlic. Remove 1½ cups of this mixture and transfer to a separate bowl (you'll add this to the gumbo toward the end). Set both bowls aside.

2. In a large bowl, combine 8 cups of filtered water, 2 tablespoons of the parsley, the oregano, thyme, canned tomatoes, fresh tomatoes, mustard, tomato paste, tamari, Worcestershire sauce, liquid smoke, vinegar, wine, and jalapeño, if using. Mix until well combined. Set aside.

3. Now you are ready to make the roux! In a large clean, well-greased cast-iron skillet (be sure to wipe out any residue), heat the peanut oil over medium-high heat. Once it's hot, add the flour and stir constantly with a large wooden spatula until it is well combined. Reduce the heat to medium and continue stirring until the roux is dark brown, 15 to 20 minutes. The goal here is to toast the flour and oil while preventing the mixture from burning. You do this by moving the flour and oil mixture constantly. If you stop for only a moment, the roux will burn and you will have to start over.

4. Reduce the heat to medium-low and add the larger amount of the onion mixture (not the reserved 1½ cups). Continue cooking, stirring constantly, until the vegetables are soft, 5 to 7 minutes.

5. Add the Creole spice blend and mix well. Cook for another 5 to 7 minutes, stirring frequently. Now you have the base of your gumbo!

1 cup peanut oil

1¼ cups all-purpose flour

Creole Spice Blend (page 250)

4 ears corn, kernels cut from the cobs, cobs reserved

6 to 8 bay leaves, depending on size and desired amount

½ cup chopped green onions, plus some for garnish

Sea salt and freshly cracked black pepper

2 to 3 cups chopped okra, or desired amount

Olive oil, for drizzling

3 to 4 cups cooked rice, for serving

6. Transfer the base to a large stockpot. Add the broth mixture, corn cobs, and the bay leaves. Mix well and bring to a boil, stirring often to prevent the bottom from burning. Once at a boil, reduce the heat to low and simmer for 40 minutes, stirring occasionally, to reduce and thicken the gumbo.

7. Add the green onions, remaining ½ cup parsley, and the reserved 1½ cups onion mixture. Simmer for another 20 minutes. If desired, add 1 to 2 cups water to loosen the gumbo. Give the gumbo a taste and season with salt and pepper. Feel free to add more cayenne pepper at this point to make it spicy as well.

8. In a skillet, combine the corn kernels and chopped okra and drizzle with olive oil. Set over medium heat and cook, stirring frequently, until the corn is golden and the okra is bright green and slightly browned, 10 to 15 minutes. Season with salt and pepper to taste.

9. To serve, ladle the gumbo into serving bowls, avoiding any bay leaves or corncobs. Add a small scoop of cooked rice on top and garnish with the cooked corn kernels, okra, and chopped parsley and green onions.

lagniappe: *Black-eyed peas and corn go together famously. They love hanging out together. I suggest you throw some in for a fun variation, making this gumbo even more hearty and delicious. Simply add cooked black-eyed peas when you add the broth mixture. Easy-peasy! (Pun intended.)*

rice

—

There are many different ways to cook rice: on the stovetop, in a rice cooker, or you can even bake it tightly covered in the oven. Restaurants often cook rice this way—it's a great method for large batches. You can also boil rice until it's partially cooked (like cooking pasta al dente) and then spread it on a baking sheet to finish in the oven. The result is perfectly cooked rice with separate, fluffy grains. I've tried cooking rice all of these ways and I must admit that I keep coming back to my tried-and-true rice cooker. The rice comes out great every time!

With regard to soaking and rinsing, I'm an advocate of both. I love the ritual of soaking my rice either the night before or in the morning and rinsing it thoroughly. Soaking reduces the amount of phytic acid, which can be difficult to digest, and it also shortens the cooking time. But, it requires some advance planning, so I leave that decision up to you. The only requirement is that you rinse the rice thoroughly—until the water runs clear—before you cook it to remove the excess starch.

My next rule of thumb is an important one, so listen up: Flavor your rice. Plain rice is the perfect blank canvas to fill with beautiful depth of flavor. At a bare minimum, a splash of rice vinegar, a pinch of sea salt, and a bay leaf or two will make plain boring rice into a dish with life.

These next few recipes are my favorite ways to infuse delicious flavor into rice. Feel free to try your own combinations of spices and herbs. When using onions, garlic, and vegetables, make sure to mince them finely so they can cook evenly with the rice.

basmati cumin rice

SERVES 2 TO 4

This side of rice is packed with flavor and is the perfect topping for chili or any Mexican- or Indian-inspired dish. The buttery basmati rice pairs perfectly with the robust, earthy flavor of cumin. Chipotle chili powder and bay leaves provide a tickle of spice.

1 cup white basmati rice

1½ cups filtered water

4 dried or 2 fresh bay leaves

1 to 2 garlic cloves, finely minced

1 tablespoon vegetable oil

1 tablespoon nutritional yeast (optional)

1 tablespoon ground cumin

1 teaspoon tamari

1 teaspoon rice vinegar

1 teaspoon sea salt

¼ teaspoon chipotle chili powder

¼ teaspoon ground turmeric

1. Place the rice in a fine-mesh sieve and rinse thoroughly with hot water until the water drains clear. Drain thoroughly and place the rice in a rice cooker or a small pot.

2. Add the water, bay leaves, garlic, vegetable oil, nutritional yeast, if using, cumin, tamari, vinegar, sea salt, chipotle powder, and turmeric and mix well. For the rice cooker, close and cook as you would normally. For stovetop, follow the package instructions for cooking time.

3. Once the rice is done, remove from the heat. Uncover, fluff the rice with a fork, and place the lid back on. Let sit for at least 5 minutes. Discard the bay leaves and serve.

creole rice

SERVES 2 TO 4

This rice has the perfect combination of Creole seasonings and spices to accompany any savory dish. The small amount of minced celery, bell peppers, and garlic become tender while cooking, infusing their delicate freshness into the grains. This rice is particularly good on top of gumbo or as a side with roasted vegetables.

1 cup long-grain white rice

1½ cups filtered water

2 tablespoons good-quality olive oil

2 tablespoons minced onion or shallot

1 garlic clove, minced

3 dried bay leaves

1 tablespoon minced celery

½ tablespoon minced red bell pepper

½ tablespoon minced green bell pepper

1 teaspoon tamari or coconut aminos

½ teaspoon dried parsley

½ teaspoon dried thyme

½ teaspoon dried oregano

¼ teaspoon sea salt, plus more to taste

⅛ teaspoon sweet paprika

⅛ teaspoon cayenne pepper

⅛ teaspoon freshly cracked black pepper, plus more to taste

1. Place the rice in a fine-mesh sieve and rinse thoroughly with hot water until the water drains clear. Drain thoroughly and place the rice into a rice cooker or small pot.

2. Add the water, the olive oil, onion, garlic, bay leaves, celery, bell peppers, tamari, parsley, thyme, oregano, sea salt, paprika, cayenne, and black pepper. For the rice cooker, close and cook as you would normally. For the stovetop, follow the package instructions.

3. Once done, remove from the heat, uncover, fluff the rice with a fork, replace the lid, and let sit for 5 minutes. Add more sea salt and pepper to taste. Discard the bay leaves and serve.

lemon herb rice

SERVES 4

Fresh lemon juice and zest can bring almost any recipe to life, especially rice. It adds a tangy and refreshing pop. In this recipe, the lemon combined with a liberal amount of chopped fresh herbs creates a fragrant side dish perfect for brothy soups and stewed chickpeas, or to serve with piping-hot steamed vegetables.

1 cup long-grain white rice

1½ cups filtered water

2 tablespoons good olive oil

2 tablespoons minced shallots

1 tablespoon minced garlic

1 green onion, chopped

1 tablespoon minced celery

1 heaping tablespoon chopped fresh basil

1 heaping tablespoon chopped fresh thyme

1 heaping tablespoon chopped fresh oregano

1 heaping tablespoon chopped fresh parsley

1 heaping tablespoon chopped fresh marjoram (optional)

3 dried bay leaves

½ teaspoon grated lemon zest

2 tablespoons fresh lemon juice

½ teaspoon sea salt, or to taste

½ teaspoon freshly cracked black pepper, or to taste

1. Place the rice in a fine-mesh sieve and rinse thoroughly with hot water until the water drains clear. Drain thoroughly and place the rice into a rice cooker or small pot.

2. Add the water, the olive oil, shallots, garlic, green onion, celery, basil, thyme, oregano, parsley, marjoram, if using, bay leaves, lemon zest, lemon juice, salt, and pepper and mix well. For the rice cooker, close and cook as you would normally. For the stovetop, follow the package instructions.

3. Remove from the heat, uncover, fluff the rice with a fork, replace the lid, and let sit for at least 5 minutes.

4. Season with more sea salt and black pepper to taste, if needed. Serve immediately.

lagniappe: *Make sure to use fresh herbs, as they offer a more vibrant flavor than their dried counterparts. Their bright green color also make this rice side particularly pleasing to the eye.*

umami rice

SERVES 4 TO 6

This rice is an umami explosion in the mouth. What I mean by that is the flavor is rich and savory and makes your taste buds incredibly happy and satisfied. Now, I know there are a few odd ingredients like ume plum vinegar and shiitake mushroom powder, but they truly elevate the dish. The ume plum vinegar provides a salty and delightfully sour tang that can be quite intense on its own but is beautifully diffused when cooked with rice. The shiitake mushroom powder is rich in glutamic acid, which creates umami. You can make your own shiitake powder by blending up dried shiitakes in a blender and storing in a tightly sealed jar. I particularly like the smoky flavor of the Korean chili flakes, but you can absolutely use regular red pepper flakes, for just a hint of spice. Toasted sesame seeds, onion, and garlic round out the flavor of this utterly delectable rice.

---

2 cups white rice, long-grain or basmati

3 tablespoons toasted sesame oil

3 tablespoons toasted sesame seeds

2 tablespoons ume plum vinegar

2 tablespoons tamari or coconut aminos

2 tablespoons nutritional yeast

1 tablespoon rice vinegar

1 tablespoon shiitake mushroom powder

1 teaspoon mellow white or chickpea miso

1 teaspoon sugar

1 teaspoon garlic powder

1 teaspoon onion powder

1 teaspoon Korean chili flakes or crushed red pepper flakes

2¾ cups filtered water

Sea salt and freshly cracked black pepper

Chopped green onions or chives, for garnish (optional)

1. Place the rice in a fine-mesh sieve and rinse thoroughly with hot water until the water drains clear. Drain thoroughly and place the rice into a rice cooker or small pot.

2. Add the sesame oil, sesame seeds, ume plum vinegar, tamari, nutritional yeast, rice vinegar, mushroom powder, miso, sugar, garlic powder, onion powder, and chili flakes to the rice and mix well. Pour in the water and mix again. For the rice cooker, close and cook as you would normally. For the stovetop, follow the package instructions for cooking time.

3. Once done, remove from the heat, uncover, fluff the rice with a fork, replace the lid, and let sit for 5 minutes. Add sea salt and black pepper to taste. Serve garnished with the green onions, if desired.

dirty rice

with smoky baked tofu

SERVES 4 TO 6

Dirty rice is most common in southern parts of Louisiana and has become popular throughout the South. Traditionally, it's made with white rice that is seasoned with Creole spices, celery, bell peppers, and onion. The dark or "dirty" color comes from small, browned bits of chicken liver or giblets, but I've replaced the meat with tofu that's pumped up with rich flavor from tamari, nutritional yeast, and tangy Worcestershire. The liquid smoke makes the tofu taste incredibly similar to meat. It's a subtle ingredient on its own, but crumbled, browned with oil, and tossed with heavily seasoned rice? You betcha ya, Mama, it's gonna be good!

---

smoky baked tofu

One 14-ounce block extra-firm tofu, drained

2 tablespoons olive oil

2 tablespoons tamari

2 tablespoons nutritional yeast

2 teaspoons vegan Worcestershire sauce

1 teaspoon liquid smoke

rice

3 tablespoons tamari

2 tablespoons extra virgin olive oil

2 tablespoons nutritional yeast

1 tablespoon rice vinegar

1 tablespoon vegan Worcestershire sauce

1 tablespoon fresh lemon juice

2 teaspoons dried parsley

1 teaspoon liquid smoke

1 teaspoon sugar

1 teaspoon smoked paprika

1 teaspoon onion powder

1 teaspoon garlic powder

1. Preheat the oven to 350°F. Line a baking sheet with parchment paper.

2. **Make the tofu:** Cut the tofu into small, bite-size cubes and place in a bowl. Toss in the olive oil, tamari, nutritional yeast, Worcestershire, and liquid smoke. Mix well. Spread the tofu onto the lined baking sheet and bake until firm and chewy, about 30 minutes. Chop into bite-size pieces. Set aside.

3. **Make the rice:** In a rice cooker or small pot, combine the tamari, olive oil, nutritional yeast, vinegar, Worcestershire sauce, lemon juice, parsley, liquid smoke, sugar, paprika, onion powder, garlic powder, thyme, celery seeds, cayenne, white pepper, sage, sea salt, and black pepper. Mix into a smooth paste.

4. Place the rice in a fine-mesh sieve and rinse thoroughly with hot water until the water runs clear. Add the rice to the rice cooker or pot along with the bay leaves and water and mix well. For the rice cooker, close and cook as you would normally. For the stovetop, follow the package instructions for cooking time. Set aside.

1 teaspoon dried thyme

1 teaspoon celery seeds

½ teaspoon cayenne pepper

½ teaspoon ground white pepper

½ teaspoon rubbed sage

½ teaspoon sea salt

½ teaspoon freshly cracked
    black pepper

2 cups long-grain white rice

6 to 8 bay leaves

3 cups filtered water

to finish

3 tablespoons extra-virgin
    olive oil

2 cups chopped onions

1 cup diced green bell pepper

1 cup diced celery

½ cup sliced green onions,
    plus more for garnish

¼ cup diced garlic

Chopped fresh parsley,
    for garnish

5. To finish: In a large pot, heat the olive oil over medium heat. Throw in the onions, bell pepper, celery, green onions, and garlic. Cook until the veggies are soft and the onions are slightly golden brown, 7 to 10 minutes. Add the chopped tofu and rice. Cook for another 10 minutes. Serve garnished with the green onions and parsley.

dirty rice–stuffed peppers

with cheesy herbed breadcrumb topping

SERVES 6

My mama would make stuffed peppers when I was a kid and they were oh so good. This dish is inspired by her recipe. Recently, she told me she knew someone who would use leftover stuffed peppers for a po' boy sandwich filling. *Genius!* Anywho, dirty rice is a great side dish on its own. But stuff it into colorful peppers and top with cheesy herbed breadcrumbs and you have a savory, juicy, and undeniably satisfying meal that's almost too pretty to eat. *Almost.*

peppers

6 large bell peppers, seeded and
   tops cut off just under the stem

2 tablespoons olive oil

Sea salt

breadcrumb topping

2 cups diced stale bread

½ cup shredded vegan
   mozzarella-style cheese

2 tablespoons olive oil

1 tablespoon fresh lemon juice

1 tablespoon nutritional yeast

½ teaspoon dried thyme

½ teaspoon dried parsley

Dash cayenne pepper

Sea salt

filling

½ batch Dirty Rice (page 164)

One 14.5-ounce can fire-roasted
   diced tomatoes

1 cup diced vegan mozzarella-
   style cheese

¼ cup nutritional yeast

Sea salt and black pepper

Sliced green onions, for garnish

Sage leaves, for garnish (optional)

1. Preheat the oven to 400°F.

2. Prepare the peppers: Place the seeded peppers cut side up on a baking sheet. Drizzle with the oil, sprinkle with the salt, and gently rub all over. Bake for 20 minutes. Remove from the oven and drain any excess liquid that has accumulated at the bottom of the peppers. Set aside to cool. Leave the oven on but reduce the temperature to 350°F.

3. Make the breadcrumb topping: Arrange the stale bread on a baking sheet and toast in the oven for 10 minutes. Remove and let cool. Add the bread to a food processor along with the mozzarella, olive oil, lemon juice, nutritional yeast, thyme, parsley, cayenne, and salt and black pepper to taste. Blitz until it's crumbly in texture. Leave the oven on.

4. Make the filling: In a large bowl, combine the dirty rice, canned tomatoes, mozzarella, and nutritional yeast and mix well. Season with salt and pepper to taste.

5. To assemble the peppers, pack them tightly with the filling. Mound the breadcrumb topping on top of each stuffed pepper and place them in a small baking dish. Bake for 30 minutes. Remove from the oven and let stand for 15 minutes. Serve garnished with the green onions and sage leaves, if desired.

lagniappe: *If you'd like to stuff 12 peppers, you can easily double this recipe and use one full batch of Dirty Rice.*

slow-cooked red beans & rice

SERVES 6 TO 8

This Louisiana recipe became a tradition for housewives to make on Mondays in the nineteenth century when they did laundry by hand. The idea was to make a dish that needed little attention and that would be perfectly cooked by the end of the day. And that's the key here: The longer this dish cooks, the creamier and richer it becomes. My first introduction to red beans was in the cafeteria at my small elementary school in Gulfport, Mississippi. The kitchen staff was made up of about seven women, and they were incredible. Everyone raved about their food—the students, the teachers, and even the parents. I remember diving into their creamy red beans, filled with bay leaves and spices. They were always served with a hot buttered roll, which I'd stuff more red beans and rice into (I know, I'm a true artist).

Since going vegan, I figured out an animal-free combination of ingredients that gives these beans the same depth of flavor as when you cook them with smoked sausage or ham. To replace the subtle sweetness, spices, and smokiness of the meat, I've added liquid smoke, soy sauce, maple syrup, and an extra kick of herbs and spices. The fresh and dried herbs, extra bay leaves, and shiitake mushrooms give this dish its richness. The final trick is to blend some of the cooked beans and add them back to the pot. This creates the creamy texture I grew up loving so much. You certainly don't have to do it that way, but I do. To help break down the hard-to-digest starches in the beans, I recommend soaking them in boiled water. For best results, soak overnight (or at least 8 hours). Some people cook their beans all day—I recommend a good 4 hours to get them nice and soft.

1 pound dried red beans, sorted and rinsed

⅓ cup olive oil

1 medium onion, chopped

3 cups roughly chopped shiitake mushroom caps

1 cup chopped celery

1 cup chopped green bell pepper

1 cup diced carrots

½ cup quartered cherry tomatoes

¼ cup minced garlic

3 tablespoons nutritional yeast

1 tablespoon onion powder

1. Add the rinsed beans to a large pot with enough water to cover them a few inches (do not add salt). Turn the heat on high and cover. Once it comes to a boil, remove from the heat and soak, covered, overnight. When ready to cook, rinse well, drain, and set aside.

2. In a large pot, heat the olive oil over medium heat. Add the onion and mushrooms and cook until soft and caramelized, 5 to 7 minutes. Reduce the heat to medium-low and add the celery, bell pepper, carrots, tomatoes, and garlic. Cook for another 10 minutes. Add the nutritional yeast, onion powder, garlic powder, maple syrup, liquid smoke, sage, thyme

recipe and ingredients continue

recipe continued from previous page

1 tablespoon garlic powder

1 tablespoon maple syrup

1 teaspoon liquid smoke, plus more to taste

2 teaspoons minced fresh sage

1 teaspoon chopped fresh thyme + 1 teaspoon dried

1 teaspoon chopped fresh oregano + 1 teaspoon dried

1 teaspoon smoked paprika

½ teaspoon ground cumin

½ teaspoon freshly cracked black pepper, or to taste

¼ teaspoon cayenne pepper

8 cups filtered water

5 dried bay leaves

2 tablespoons tamari or soy sauce

1 teaspoon sea salt, or to taste

⅓ cup peanut oil

Cooked rice, for serving

½ cup chopped fresh parsley, for garnish

½ cup sliced green onions, for garnish

Louisiana hot sauce, for serving (optional)

(both fresh and dried), oregano (fresh and dried), smoked paprika, cumin, black pepper, and cayenne. Cook for another 5 minutes, or until the mixture smells outrageously good.

3. Add the water, drained beans, and bay leaves to the pot and bring to a rapid boil. Boil for a solid 5 minutes. Reduce the heat to medium-low and simmer for 2 hours, stirring occasionally to make sure the bottom doesn't burn. After 2 hours, add 1 to 2 cups more water as needed to create a thick gravy texture. Add the tamari and sea salt. Taste the beans and add more if needed. Cook until the beans are soft, an additional hour. Remove the bay leaves.

4. Once the beans are soft, transfer 2 cups to a food processor and blend. With the machine running, drizzle in the peanut oil and scrape down the sides as needed. Continue until the beans are smooth and creamy. Transfer this mixture back to the pot and mix well. Serve as is or continue to cook over low heat, stirring occasionally, for as long as you'd like, adding more water when needed.

5. To serve, scoop the beans into a bowl and plop one scoop of rice on top. Sprinkle with the fresh parsley and sliced green onions. Serve with Louisiana hot sauce, if desired.

lagniappe: *I recommend adding salt to the beans at the very end of the cooking process to ensure the beans become soft and creamy. Adding salt early on may make the beans tough. You can use canned red beans if you would like, but that goes against everything I believe in (my mama would agree).*

toasted popcorn rice with pecans

SERVES 4 TO 6

If you can ever get your hands on Louisiana popcorn rice, you will be delighted by its intoxicating buttery and nutty aroma (hence the name). You can find it in grocery stores throughout southern Louisiana and you can easily order it in bulk online (which I did when I lived in New York City). Toasting the rice and pecans brings out their rich flavor, while sweet, crunchy carrots and grassy celery make this dish truly delectable.

½ cup chopped pecans

2 cups Louisiana popcorn rice or long-grain white rice

2 or 3 large dried bay leaves

1 tablespoon nutritional yeast

½ teaspoon sea salt, or to taste

¼ teaspoon freshly cracked black pepper, or to taste

Dash ground turmeric

Dash cayenne pepper (optional)

2 tablespoons minced carrots

2 tablespoons minced celery

1 tablespoon fresh lemon juice or rice vinegar

2 tablespoons cold-pressed pecan oil or olive oil

3 cups filtered water

Thinly sliced green onions, for garnish

1. Heat a large pan or skillet over medium heat. Add the pecans and dry-toast for a few minutes, until fragrant, stirring constantly with a wooden spatula. Remove and set aside.

2. Add the rice to the pan and dry-toast, stirring constantly, until the rice begins to turn golden brown and you notice a nutty aroma. Toward the end, add the nutritional yeast and toast for an additional minute. Transfer the rice and nutritional yeast to a rice cooker or small pot.

3. Add the salt, pepper, turmeric, cayenne, carrots, celery, lemon juice, oil, and water to the rice mixture. Stir and mix well.

4. For the rice cooker, close and cook as you would normally. For the stovetop, follow the package instructions for cooking time. Once done, turn off the heat, uncover, fluff the rice with a fork, replace the lid, and let sit for at least 5 minutes.

5. To serve, chop the toasted pecans and sprinkle on top along with the green onions.

lagniappe: *Dry-toasting means to heat a skillet over medium heat without any oil and then cook the ingredient in the dry pan until toasted. You can do this to toast nuts, seeds, and spices as well. When you are dry-toasting, always make sure the pan is clean and free from residue so that it does not burn and ruin whatever you are toasting!*

mississippi macro bowl

with creamy pink beans

MAKES ABOUT 6 MACRO BOWLS

This dish is my version of a Mississippi-style macro bowl. I mean, slow-cooked beans, cornbread, collard greens, sweet potatoes, and hot sauce? You really can't get more Mississippi than that! (Aside from the fact that it's healthy! Ha!) The concept of a macro bowl is to create a balanced mix of grains, protein, vegetables (raw and cooked), beans, a healthy fat, and sometimes a sea vegetable and/or fermented food. The sky's the limit, really. You can add a handful of raw nuts or seeds, avocado, sauerkraut, or kimchi, and maybe a sprinkling of dried seaweed. Just remember to have fun and be creative. The ultimate goal is to create a feel-good dish that is nutrient-dense, wholesome, and filling.

---

creamy pink beans

1 pound pink beans, sorted and rinsed

One 2-inch piece kombu

6 dried bay leaves

¼ cup vegetable oil

1 large onion, chopped

2 tablespoons chopped garlic

1 tablespoon onion powder

1 tablespoon garlic powder

1 teaspoon liquid smoke

1 teaspoon sugar

½ teaspoon ground cumin

¼ teaspoon cayenne pepper

10 cups filtered water

¼ cup good olive oil

2 tablespoons tamari

Sea salt

1. **Make the creamy pink beans:** Bring a large pot of water to boil (do not add any salt). Add the beans, kombu, and bay leaves. Bring to a boil and boil for a solid 5 minutes. Remove from the heat, cover, and set aside for at least 1 hour. Once soaked, drain the beans, removing the kombu and bay leaves, and rinse thoroughly.

2. Add the vegetable oil to the same pot and heat over medium heat. Add the onion and cook until soft and caramelized, about 10 minutes. Add the garlic and cook, stirring constantly to prevent burning, until soft and caramelized, an additional 10 minutes. Add the onion powder, garlic powder, liquid smoke, sugar, cumin, and cayenne. Mix well. Add the drained beans and the water. Cover and bring to a rapid boil. Once at a rapid boil, cook for 5 minutes. Uncover, reduce the heat to medium-low, and cook for 1½ hours, stirring occasionally to prevent burning.

3. Once the beans are tender, add about 1 cup of beans and the olive oil to a small blender and blend until smooth and creamy. Return the blended mixture to the pot. Add the tamari and sea salt to taste and reduce the heat to low. Continue to cook, stirring frequently, until the beans are

assembly

2 small sweet potatoes,
cut into ⅓-inch-thick rounds
(about 3 cups)

Sea salt

Creole Rice (page 160),
for serving

Sautéed Collard Greens
(page 198) or Skillet Okra
(page 225), for serving

Skillet Cornbread (page 55),
for serving

Meyer Lemon Miso-Tahini
Dressing (page 113) or
Creamy Maple Mustard
Dressing (page 117),
for serving

Homemade Hot Sauce
(page 267), for serving

tender, thick, and creamy, an additional 15 to 20 minutes. If the beans are too thick, add more water if desired.

4. Meanwhile, preheat the oven to 375°F. Line a baking sheet with parchment paper.

5. Spread the sweet potatoes across the baking sheet. Coat with vegetable oil spray and sprinkle with sea salt. Flip and repeat. Bake until tender, about 20 minutes.

6. To assemble the bowls, add one scoop each of the beans, rice, sweet potatoes, and collard greens. Serve with one piece of cornbread, a side or drizzle of the dressing, and a side of the hot sauce.

southern spanakopita

MAKES ONE PIE (8 LARGE PIECES)

Spanakopita was one of the first recipes I made when I first became vegan. I'm not exactly sure why but I think it's because it's usually the recipe featured on the box of phyllo dough. Every time I saw that shot of spinach pie with crumbled feta, I thought to myself, "That looks kind of like tofu." (If that's not the most vegan thing you've ever heard, I don't know what is . . . .) So, I started making spanakopita: sautéed onions, garlic, and spinach with buttery pine nuts, loads of seasonings and spices, and, of course, crumbled tofu for that lovely feta texture, all wrapped in multiple layers of crispy, golden phyllo dough. The secret ingredient is just a touch of nutmeg. Now, since moving back to the 'Sip, I have an abundance of collard greens. So, I swapped out the spinach for that and guess what? It's perfectly delicious.

---

2 tablespoons + ½ cup good cold-pressed olive oil

2 cups chopped onions

¼ cup chopped garlic

8 cups packed shredded collard greens (about 3 bunches)

1 cup chopped green onions

¾ cup finely chopped fresh dill, plus sprigs for garnish

One 14-ounce package extra-firm tofu, crumbled and drained

¾ cup pine nuts

3 tablespoons nutritional yeast (optional), plus more for sprinkling

2 tablespoons white wine vinegar

2 tablespoons mellow white miso or chickpea miso

2 tablespoons fresh lemon juice, plus lemon slices for garnish

1 teaspoon onion powder

1 teaspoon garlic powder

1 teaspoon sea salt, or to taste, plus more for sprinkling

1. In a skillet, heat 2 tablespoons of olive oil over medium heat. Add the onions and garlic and cook until soft and caramelized, about 5 minutes. Add the collard greens and cook until wilted, about 5 minutes. Add the green onions and dill and cook for another 5 minutes. Drain any excess liquid and transfer to a large bowl. Add the tofu, pine nuts, nutritional yeast, if using, vinegar, miso, lemon juice, onion powder, garlic powder, salt, black pepper, nutmeg, and cayenne. Gently mix and set aside. (You want the tofu to look similar to crumbled feta.)

2. Pour the remaining ½ cup of olive oil into a small bowl for brushing the phyllo dough (add more if needed as you go along). Set aside, close to where you will assemble the pie.

3. Using a large cast-iron skillet or 9 × 13-inch baking dish, layer one sheet of phyllo dough in the pan, allowing 2 to 3 inches to drape over the edge. Brush with olive oil and add another sheet, overlapping the first. Repeat this step until all edges of the phyllo dough are covered and the bottom of the skillet or dish is covered completely, using about 12 sheets of dough altogether. This will be the bottom crust of the pie.

recipe and ingredients continue

recipe continued from previous page

½ teaspoon freshly cracked
   black pepper, or to taste

¼ teaspoon freshly grated
   nutmeg

Dash cayenne pepper

One 16-ounce box frozen phyllo
   dough (28 sheets), thawed

4. Transfer the filling to the dough-lined skillet or baking dish and spread into an even layer. Fold all of the edges of the dough toward the center of the pie and brush with olive oil. Create a top layer of dough by laying down one sheet of phyllo and folding the edges so it fits within the skillet or dish. Brush with olive oil and repeat this step until you have 10 layers. Crinkle the remaining 6 sheets (think crinkled paper) and place on top of the pie in segments, arranging them artistically until the top is covered.

5. Sprinkle with sea salt and nutritional yeast and coat thoroughly with olive oil. Chill for 30 minutes in the refrigerator. This will make it easier to score the pie.

6. Meanwhile, preheat the oven to 350°F.

7. Once chilled, score the pie into desired pieces (I recommend 8 large pieces for an entree portion). Bake until the top is golden brown, 30 to 40 minutes. Remove from the oven and let sit for 15 minutes. Slice through the scored lines and the crust and serve. Garnish with fresh dill sprigs and lemon slices.

lagniappe: *For presentation purposes, I love using my large cast-iron skillet for this dish. If you do not have one, you can use whatever baking dish you would like as long as it's at least 9 × 13 inches. You can use olive oil spray, a pastry brush, or your hands to distribute the olive oil. Crinkling the top layers of phyllo dough creates a crispy and very dramatic top to the pie.*

mushroom rigatoni casserole

with creamy garlic cheese sauce

SERVES 4

Okay, this is an all-star dish that will seriously impress. Exotic dried mushrooms create an intensely rich and earthy flavor, while the garlicky cheese sauce blankets every bite. Any baking vessel will work: a cheesecake pan, 9 × 13-inch dish, or individual ramekins. I use mini cast-iron skillets because—duh. As the casserole bakes, the noodles become crisp and golden brown on top, which gives them an irresistible texture. Now, don't roll your eyes at me when you look at the instructions. Good recipes like this take time! I mean, you see the picture. It's a showstopper. That said, set aside some time on the weekend to make this. Having a friend or a loved one helps. Wine does, too.

---

filling

1 ounce dried shiitake mushrooms

3 cups warm filtered water

1 ounce dried lobster mushrooms

1 ounce dried porcini mushrooms

½ large onion, chopped

10 garlic cloves, peeled

2 tablespoons olive oil

2 tablespoons nutritional yeast

1 tablespoon white wine vinegar

1 tablespoon tamari or coconut aminos

1 teaspoon dried thyme

½ teaspoon sea salt, or to taste

pasta

1 pound rigatoni pasta

Olive oil

1. **Make the filling:** Place all the dried mushrooms in a bowl. Pour the water over the mushrooms and place a small plate on top to keep them submerged. Set aside for 20 minutes to soften. Drain the mushrooms through a colander set over a bowl. Strain the soaking liquid through a coffee filter or fine-mesh sieve and set aside.

2. Rinse the rehydrated mushrooms, removing any grit. Transfer the mushrooms to a food processor along with the onion, garlic, olive oil, nutritional yeast, vinegar, tamari, thyme, and salt. Blend, scraping down the sides as needed, until you have a crumbly paste.

3. Transfer the mixture to a skillet and cook over medium heat, stirring occasionally, until browned, about 5 minutes. Add the reserved mushroom soaking liquid to the mushroom mixture and cook, stirring often, until the broth is completely evaporated and the mixture is a thick paste, 15 to 20 minutes.

4. Preheat the oven to 400°F.

recipe and ingredients continue

recipe continued from previous page

cheese sauce

Two 7-ounce packages sliced white vegan cheese (see lagniappe), chopped

1½ cups filtered water

½ cup raw cashews

4 garlic cloves

1 tablespoon nutritional yeast

2 teaspoons mellow white miso or chickpea miso

½ teaspoon freshly cracked black pepper

¼ teaspoon freshly grated nutmeg

Dash cayenne pepper

5. **Meanwhile, cook the pasta:** Bring a large pot of salted water to a boil. Cook the rigatoni until al dente (the pasta will cook more in the oven). Drain and transfer back to the pot. Drizzle with olive oil to prevent sticking, toss, and set aside.

6. **Make the cheese sauce:** In a blender, combine the cheese, water, cashews, garlic, nutritional yeast, miso, black pepper, nutmeg, and cayenne and blend until smooth, scraping down the sides as needed.

7. Pour a little bit of the cheese sauce to cover the bottom of the desired baking vessel(s). Stack the rigatoni upright, like little soldiers, into the vessel. Spread the mushroom mixture over the top and press it down into the rigatoni cavities. Pour the cheese sauce over everything and bake until the top of the bake is golden brown, about 30 minutes. Let stand for 10 minutes and serve.

lagniappe: *I've been pleasantly surprised to find unique dried mushrooms at most common grocery stores. You just have to look for them or ask. You can also find them at most specialty food stores or order them online. The best part about dried mushrooms is they have a very long shelf life and they are packed with flavor. Some are grittier than others, especially the wild ones, so I always recommend soaking and rinsing them and straining their broth through a coffee filter or fine-mesh sieve. As for the cheese, you can go with provolone, smoked gouda, or mozzarella-style slices.*

eggplant couscous casserole

SERVES 4 TO 6

This dish is inspired by a dinner my longtime friend Tyler once made for me. He is a fabulous cook, and we met when we were both living in Charleston, South Carolina. He actually lived with me for a short while, and I always remember him bringing home an abundance of fresh vegetables: plump eggplants, bright sweet bell peppers, huge sweet potatoes, and loads of onions and garlic. I happily benefited from his love of cooking! One night, I watched him make a dish with eggplant and couscous. He placed plump eggplant halves that were scored deeply with X's on top of a bed of couscous. After loading the dish up with more vegetables like peppers and onions, he poured over richly seasoned vegetable broth and baked it in the oven. I remember how tender the eggplant became, the insides caramelized and creamy. The couscous had absorbed all of the beautiful juices and flavors of the fresh herbs, garlic, and onions. One day my CSA delivery contained all the ingredients for the dish, and I instantly remembered when he made it for me. I just knew I had to make my own version and share the recipe. Tyler, this one's for you.

One 10-ounce box couscous (1½ cups)

2 to 3 medium (or 1 very large) eggplants, halved lengthwise and scored in a diamond pattern

6 ounces baby carrots

6 ounces sweet potato, peeled and cut into 1-inch chunks

3 ounces bell pepper, sliced into rings

1 small onion (3 to 4 ounces), sliced

2 cups filtered water

¼ cup olive oil

¼ cup chopped garlic

2 tablespoons nutritional yeast

2 tablespoons tamari or coconut aminos

1 tablespoon mellow white miso or chickpea miso

1. Preheat the oven to 350°F.

2. Spread the uncooked couscous onto the bottom of a 9 × 13-inch baking dish. Place the eggplant on top of the couscous. Place the carrots, sweet potatoes, and bell peppers in between the gaps.

3. In a medium bowl, whisk together the onion, water, olive oil, garlic, nutritional yeast, tamari, miso, oregano, thyme, parsley, vinegar, onion powder, garlic powder, salt, black pepper, and cayenne and pour over the couscous mixture.

recipe and ingredients continue

1 tablespoon chopped fresh
oregano

1 tablespoon chopped fresh
thyme

1 tablespoon chopped fresh
parsley, plus more for garnish

2 teaspoons rice vinegar

2 teaspoons onion powder

2 teaspoons garlic powder

1 teaspoon sea salt,
or to taste

½ teaspoon freshly cracked
black pepper

¼ teaspoon cayenne pepper

4. Wrap the baking dish tightly with foil and bake for 30 minutes. Remove from the oven and gently mix everything. Turn the temperature up to 450°F, return to the oven, and roast until the sweet potatoes are tender, an additional 25 minutes. Serve garnished with fresh parsley.

lagniappe: *When scoring the eggplant, go deep but not all the way through so that the eggplant stays intact. If you don't have fresh herbs, you can substitute the dried variety.*

spaghetti pie

with summer squash

SERVES 6 TO 8

I remember the first time I had spaghetti pie when I was a little kid. My friend's mother made it for us, and I was obsessed with the fact that it was a pie made out of noodles. It still excites me just thinking about it, which is why I make it to this day. The best part? When someone looks at you like you're crazy and says, "Spaghetti pie!?" I love adding summer squash or zucchini to make this dish juicy. As for my "easy marinara?" Well, it really is. You should have everything in your pantry to whip it up in no time. Simply doctor up 2 cans of fire-roasted tomatoes and there you have it. Easy breezy.

easy marinara

2 tablespoons olive oil

1 medium red onion, chopped

¼ cup chopped garlic

Two 14.5-ounce cans fire-roasted diced tomatoes

1 teaspoon onion powder

1 teaspoon garlic powder

½ teaspoon dried basil

½ teaspoon dried oregano

½ teaspoon dried rosemary

½ teaspoon dried thyme

½ teaspoon sugar (optional)

Dash freshly grated nutmeg

Crushed red pepper flakes

Chopped fresh herbs, if you got 'em

Salt and freshly cracked black pepper

1. Preheat the oven to 350°F. Grease a 7-inch springform pan or pie dish.

2. **Make the easy marinara:** In a small pot, heat the olive oil over medium heat. Toss in the onion and cook until tender, about 10 minutes. Add the garlic and cook until tender, about 5 minutes. Add the tomatoes, onion powder, garlic powder, basil, oregano, rosemary, thyme, sugar, nutmeg, pepper flakes, and fresh herbs, if using, and bring to a boil. Reduce the heat to low and simmer, stirring occasionally, for about 20 minutes. Season with salt and pepper to taste. For a smoother marinara, blend with an immersion blender or in a stand blender.

recipe and ingredients continue

recipe continued from previous page

spaghetti pie

½ cup nutritional yeast, plus more for sprinkling

2 tablespoons potato starch

2 tablespoons olive oil

One 16-ounce package spaghetti, cooked according to package directions

8 ounces yellow squash, sliced into ¼-inch-thick rounds (2 to 3 squash)

¼ cup breadcrumbs

Sea salt and freshly cracked black pepper

Vegan parmesan-style shreds, for garnish (optional)

3. **Make the pie:** In a bowl, combine the marinara (reserving some for the top), nutritional yeast, potato starch, and olive oil. Mix well. Toss in the cooked spaghetti and sliced squash and mix until thoroughly incorporated. Transfer to the greased pan or dish and squoosh down the mixture. Spoon on remaining marinara in the middle and spread into a thin layer, leaving some noodles exposed for the crust. Sprinkle with breadcrumbs, nutritional yeast, and sea salt and pepper to taste.

4. Bake until the edges are crispy, 20 to 30 minutes. Slice and serve with vegan Parmesan, if desired.

blueberry bbq tempeh

with fingerling potatoes, collard greens & horseradish cream sauce

SERVES 4

Did you know that blueberries can make a fantastic and unique touch to savory recipes? Like BBQ! I make a rich sauce with fresh blueberries and loads of seasonings and spices. My favorite part is the beautiful purple hue that's created once the sauce is cooked down. This recipe stars my famous blueberry BBQ sauce while truly merging my past and my present. The first time I had BBQ tempeh was at my dear friend Pamela's restaurant, Blossom, in Chelsea in New York City. It was a dish with large, plump triangles of tempeh, roasted potatoes, sautéed collard greens, and a rich horseradish cream sauce—a flavor combination that's truly outstanding. This recipe is my very own twist on that memorable meal.

---

potatoes

1½ pounds fingerling potatoes, rinsed and quartered lengthwise

2 tablespoons vegetable oil

½ teaspoon sea salt, or to taste

½ teaspoon freshly cracked black pepper, or to taste

1 tablespoon nutritional yeast (optional)

bbq tempeh

Two 8-ounce packages plain tempeh, cut into bite-size strips

Blueberry BBQ Sauce (page 260)

horseradish cream sauce

1 cup raw cashews

¾ cup filtered water

3 tablespoons prepared horseradish

1 tablespoon vegetable oil

1 teaspoon fresh lemon juice

½ teaspoon sea salt, or to taste

for serving

Sautéed Collard Greens (page 198)

1. Preheat the oven to 350°F. Line a baking sheet with parchment paper.

2. **Prepare the potatoes:** Place the potatoes, oil, sea salt, black pepper, and nutritional yeast, if using, on the baking sheet and toss together. Bake until the potatoes are tender and crispy on the edges, about 1 hour. Check them at about 45 minutes to see where they are at.

3. **Make the BBQ tempeh:** Arrange the tempeh in a single layer in a 9 × 13-inch baking dish. Pour on the BBQ sauce to cover it completely. Wrap tightly with foil and bake for 30 minutes. Take out and remove the foil. Flip the tempeh and bake, uncovered, for an additional 30 minutes.

4. **Make the horseradish cream sauce:** In a blender, combine the cashews, water, horseradish, oil, lemon juice, and salt and blend until smooth.

5. To serve, beautifully arrange the tempeh, collards, and potatoes in serving bowls. Drizzle with the horseradish cream sauce.

blue spice basil pesto pasta

SERVES 4 TO 6

The first time I encountered blue spice basil was at the Campo Rosso Farm stand at the Union Square farmers' market in New York City. I remember buying my first bushel and being overwhelmed by its intoxicating scent. And then I tasted it: pungent, sweet, and citrusy, with an incredibly complex flavor. The best part is the flowering part of the plant. Talk about flavor town, people! Once I moved back to Mississippi, I ordered some seeds immediately. After the last frost of the winter, I planted them everywhere. When you have an abundance of fresh basil, naturally, you make pesto. And in my opinion, pesto made with blue spice is the *best*. Feel free to use whatever variety of basil you can find, but if you grow your own blue spice seeds, you'll totally get it.

½ cup blanched almonds

¼ cup nutritional yeast

2½ cups fresh blue spice basil leaves, rinsed and packed

⅓ cup fresh oregano leaves, rinsed and packed

⅓ cup fresh thyme leaves, rinsed and packed

⅓ cup fresh parsley leaves, rinsed and packed

⅓ cup fresh chives

¼ cup good olive oil

2 large or 3 small garlic cloves, roughly chopped

1 teaspoon mellow white miso

1 teaspoon grated lemon zest

2 to 3 tablespoons fresh lemon juice, to taste

½ teaspoon sugar

½ teaspoon sea salt, or to taste

½ teaspoon freshly cracked black pepper, or to taste

1 pound orecchiette pasta

1 cup frozen shelled edamame

1 cup frozen peas

1 cup sugar snap peas

1. In a skillet, combine the almonds and nutritional yeast. Cook over medium heat, stirring constantly, until the mixture is fragrant and lightly toasted, 2 to 3 minutes. Remove, let cool, and toss into a food processor along with the basil, oregano, thyme, parsley, chives, olive oil, garlic, miso, lemon zest, lemon juice, sugar, sea salt, and black pepper. Blend for a few minutes until nice and smooth, stopping occasionally to scrape down the sides. Taste a little bit and see if you'd like to add more salt, pepper, or lemon juice. Set aside.

2. Add a dash of salt to a large pot of water and bring to a boil. Cook the pasta until *almost* done (follow the instructions on the package). During the last minute, throw in the edamame, peas, and sugar snap peas. Finish cooking the pasta and the peas (don't worry, they don't need long). Drain everything thoroughly in a colander and return to the pot. Scrape in all of the pesto. Toss well. Serve garnished with black pepper and sea salt if desired. Enjoy!

salisbury steak

with mushroom onion gravy

MAKES 6 TO 8 STEAKS

I can so vividly remember eating Salisbury steak in my elementary school cafeteria. As I've mentioned before, this was no ordinary cafeteria. They really knew how to throw down! The mashed potatoes were topped with a rich well of gravy. The steak itself was like a delicious piece of meatloaf: tender, succulent, juicy, and smothered with gravy and caramelized onions. No doubt, this was one of my first introductions to comfort food. That's precisely why I knew that I had to create this recipe—to fill the empty void I felt after not having it for so many years. So here you are! This steak mixture is chock-full of seasonings, herbs, and spices and the onions cook down to become carmelized and sweet. The best part? It's a one-stop shop. All you need is a large skillet or Dutch oven. Make the patties, brown them, add some sliced onions, fresh herbs, water, and pop that sucker in the oven. Once the steaks absorb all the flavor and plump up, they're done. Then you make a gravy with all the succulent remnants left over in the pan. You'd do yourself right to serve these with mashed potatoes and some steamed green beans. Now, *that's* a meal.

---

steaks

1 cup dried TVP (textured vegetable protein)

3 tablespoons nutritional yeast

½ tablespoon onion powder

½ tablespoon garlic powder

1 teaspoon dried oregano

1 teaspoon dried thyme

1 teaspoon sea salt

1½ cups boiling water

2½ cups vital wheat gluten

½ cup + 2 tablespoons vegetable oil

¼ cup red wine

¼ cup very finely minced garlic (use a Microplane or garlic press)

1. Preheat the oven to 350°F.

2. Make the steaks: In a large bowl, combine the TVP, nutritional yeast, onion powder, garlic powder, oregano, thyme, and salt. Mix well. Pour the boiling water over the top of the mixture and let it plump up for 5 minutes.

3. Add the vital wheat gluten, ½ cup of the vegetable oil, the wine, garlic, tamari, liquid smoke, mustard, Worcestershire sauce, and pepper to taste to the bowl of the TVP mixture. Mix well and knead the dough for a good 5 minutes. Shape the dough into 6 to 8 oval-shaped steaks, adding more water if needed to help combine the dough. It's okay if some of the dough is slightly crumbly, as it will plump up and solidify while baking and any remnants will become a part of the gravy.

recipe and ingredients continue

recipe continued from previous page

2 tablespoons tamari

1 teaspoon liquid smoke

1 tablespoon whole-grain mustard

1 tablespoon vegan Worcestershire sauce

Freshly cracked black pepper

½ pound sliced cremini mushrooms

3 cups filtered water

1 large onion, thinly sliced into half-moons

5 dried bay leaves

Few sprigs fresh thyme

Few sprigs fresh parsley

3 fresh sage leaves

1 sprig fresh rosemary

mushroom onion gravy

3 tablespoons all-purpose flour

½ cup red wine

1½ cups vegetable broth or water

2 tablespoons nutritional yeast

1 tablespoon tamari

1½ teaspoons sea salt, or to taste

1 teaspoon minced fresh rosemary

Mashed Potatoes (page 210) or Creole Rice (page 160), to serve

4. In a large cast-iron skillet or Dutch oven, heat the remaining 2 tablespoons vegetable oil over medium-high heat. Add the steaks to the pan and cook until golden brown on both sides, about 5 minutes per side.

5. Pour the water over the steaks and add the mushrooms, onion, bay leaves, thyme, parsley, sage, and rosemary. Cover tightly with a double layer of foil or a lid and bake for 45 minutes. Remove the foil and bake, uncovered, for an additional 30 minutes, reducing the liquid. Remove from the oven and gently flip the patties, removing the bay leaves and herb stems. Return to the oven and bake for a final 20 minutes, or until the steaks are firm to the touch. Remove from the oven and transfer the steaks to a serving platter.

6. **Make the mushroom onion gravy:** Place the skillet back on the stovetop with the onions and mushrooms. Add the flour and cook over medium heat for about 5 minutes, stirring constantly to toast the flour. Add the red wine to deglaze the pan, stirring constantly. Add the vegetable broth, nutritional yeast, tamari, salt, and rosemary. Cook, stirring constantly, until thick and creamy.

7. Pour the gravy over the steaks and serve with rice or mashed potatoes.

lagniappe: *This recipe works beautifully as a hamburger patty base as well. Simply shape the mixture into desired patty shapes and get you some buns plus all the fixin's!*

wild chanterelle pasta

with truffled cashew cream

SERVES 4 TO 6

I created this dish after foraging for wild chanterelles one hot Mississippi summer. I'm talking I was up to my ears with these mushies! I had buckets of 'em! My go-to with wild mushrooms is always to eat them lightly fried with some olive oil, sea salt, and pepper. But that's not really a recipe, is it, y'all? So I decided to create a cashew cream that would work perfectly tossed with angel hair noodles and crispy mushrooms. If you can't source chanterelles, use shiitakes. The white truffle oil and sprinkling of truffle salt make this a sensual dish. It's one to make for your boo or someone that you want to *be* your boo. You get the idea.

truffled cashew cream

2 cups filtered water

1 cup raw cashews

2 tablespoons nutritional yeast

1 tablespoon fresh lemon juice

½ teaspoon sea salt

Dash freshly grated nutmeg

Freshly cracked black pepper

pasta

16 ounces angel hair pasta

Sea salt

Olive oil

1. **Make the truffled cashew cream:** In a high-powered blender, combine the water, cashews, nutritional yeast, lemon juice, sea salt, nutmeg, and pepper to taste and blend until smooth.

2. **Make the pasta:** Bring a large pot of water with a healthy amount of salt to a boil. Cook the pasta according to package instructions until al dente (keep in mind that the pasta will continue to cook). Remove at least 1 cup of the pasta water to use later and drain the pasta. Return the pasta to the pot, toss with a drizzle of olive oil, cover, and set aside.

3. **Make the mushrooms:** In a large cast-iron skillet, heat the olive oil over medium-high heat. Add the mushrooms and cook, stirring occasionally, until the edges start to brown slightly, about 7 minutes. Remove half of the mushrooms for garnish. Reduce the heat to medium-low and add the shallots and garlic. Cook for an additional 5 to 7 minutes, until the shallots and garlic are golden brown and the remaining mushrooms are crispy.

recipe and ingredients continue

recipe continued from previous page

mushrooms

1 tablespoon olive oil

1 pound chanterelle or shiitake caps, cleaned, dried, and torn or cut into bite-size pieces

2 tablespoons diced shallot

1 tablespoon minced garlic

Sea salt, to taste

3 tablespoons truffle oil, or to taste

½ teaspoon truffle sea salt, or to taste

Fresh parsley, for garnish

4. Pour the cashew cream into the skillet with the mushrooms and stir constantly until the cashew cream begins to thicken, 5 to 7 minutes. Remove from the heat and add the pasta. Using tongs, toss the pasta until thoroughly coated. If desired, add some pasta water to loosen the sauce. Drizzle the white truffle oil on top and sprinkle on the white truffle sea salt. Place the reserved mushrooms on top and garnish with fresh parsley. Serve immediately.

lagniappe: *If the mushrooms are dirty, rinse them under running water and dry them thoroughly in a salad spinner. You want to remove all of the moisture for effective cooking.*

CHAPTER 6

—

sides

sautéed collard greens

Collard greens are a staple here in the South. A cousin of cabbage and kale, this nutrient-dense green is delicious when it is cooked until tender with the simplest of seasonings: sea salt and black pepper. I add a splash of lemon juice and rice vinegar to give it a little zip, but you could use any vinegar you desire.

---

2 tablespoons vegetable oil

8 cups shredded collard greens

1 tablespoon rice vinegar

½ teaspoon sea salt, or to taste

Freshly cracked black pepper

1 teaspoon fresh lemon juice

1. In a large cast-iron skillet, heat the vegetable oil over medium-high heat. Throw in the collard greens, rice vinegar, sea salt, and black pepper to taste. Cook, stirring frequently, until tender but still bright green in color, about 5 minutes.

2. Drizzle the lemon juice over top and serve.

crispy garlic potatoes

SERVES 4 TO 6

It's no secret that potatoes are my weakness. I'm hooked! And if you like potatoes as much as I do, this recipe is just for you. Boiling the chunks creates a succulent, juicy interior while roasting them with a savory coating gives them that crispy outside we all love. I also add a ridiculous amount of garlic because, well, I can be ridiculous sometimes. Don't worry, though, once roasted, it becomes mellow, sweet, and just downright delicious.

boiled potatoes

2 pounds russet potatoes, peeled and cut in 1½-inch chunks

3 tablespoons distilled white vinegar

1 tablespoon sugar

1 tablespoon sea salt

coating

⅓ cup minced garlic

½ cup olive oil

1 tablespoon white vinegar

1 tablespoon fresh lemon juice

⅓ cup nutritional yeast

2 tablespoons all-purpose flour

1 teaspoon sea salt

½ teaspoon freshly cracked black pepper

¼ teaspoon ground turmeric

Dash cayenne pepper

Sea salt and freshly cracked black pepper

Thinly sliced green onions, for garnish

1. Preheat the oven to 425°F.

2. **Boil the potatoes:** Add the potatoes to a large pot and fill with water. Add the vinegar, sugar, and salt. Bring to a boil and cook until fork-tender, about 20 minutes.

3. **Meanwhile, make the coating:** In a small blender or food processor, combine all the ingredients and blend until smooth. Transfer to a large bowl and set aside.

4. Once the potatoes are done, drain and transfer them to the bowl of coating. Gently toss, coating the potato chunks thoroughly.

5. Spread the potatoes evenly in a large cast-iron skillet or on a parchment-lined baking sheet. Bake until the potatoes are golden brown and crispy all around, 40 to 50 minutes, tossing every 15 minutes. Every oven is different, so keep an eye on them to make sure they don't burn! The potatoes are already cooked, so the goal here is to get a beautiful golden crust.

6. Season with salt and pepper to taste and garnish with the green onions.

cornbread dressing

with sage cracker topping

SERVES 6 TO 8

Growing up, I remember eating cornbread dressing, a moist and flavorful casserole-esque stuffing, in my school cafeteria. It was served in a mound, smothered with gravy, and the most memorable flavor component was most definitely celery. Most traditional Southern dressings are made with a turkey neck broth and often giblet gravy. Yikes! How about we leave out that cute gobbling turkey and just up the herbs and spices? Sound good? I've also figured out a way to streamline this classic side—instead of making a separate recipe of cornbread, I created a hack where you bake everything together in only one dish. Once the initial baking is done, you can store it in the fridge overnight or serve immediately. The final steps are adding fresh celery for an extra kick of freshness, vegetable broth to provide moistness, and a crunchy sage cracker topping to seal the deal.

dressing

2 cups finely ground cornmeal

1 cup whole-wheat pastry flour

2 tablespoons cornstarch

1½ teaspoons salt

1 teaspoon baking powder

½ teaspoon baking soda

Dash cayenne pepper

2 cups corn kernels, fresh or frozen (one 10-ounce bag)

2 tablespoons olive oil

2 cups chopped onion (about 1 large)

1 cup chopped celery, including leaves

1 cup diced red bell pepper

½ cup chopped garlic

¼ cup nutritional yeast

1 tablespoon onion powder

1 tablespoon garlic powder

2 teaspoons rubbed sage

1. Preheat the oven to 425°F. Grease a 9 × 13-inch baking dish and set aside.

2. **Make the dressing:** In a bowl, whisk together the cornmeal, flour, cornstarch, salt, baking powder, baking soda, and cayenne. Throw in the corn kernels, mix well, and set aside.

3. In a large skillet, heat the oil over medium heat. Throw in the onion, celery, and bell pepper. Sauté, stirring often, until everything is soft, about 5 minutes. Add the garlic and cook, stirring often, until tender, another 5 minutes. Reduce the heat to low. Add the nutritional yeast, onion powder, garlic powder, sage, and black pepper. Mix well and cook for 5 minutes. Remove from the heat, add to the flour mixture, and thoroughly combine. Set aside.

4. In a high-powdered blender, combine the cashews, water, and lemon juice and blend until smooth. (If starting with a plant-based milk, whisk it together with the lemon juice in a bowl.) Stir in the melted butter to incorporate. Pour over the batter and mix until incorporated.

½ teaspoon freshly cracked
black pepper

½ cup raw cashews plus 2 cups
filtered water (or 2½ cups plain
unsweetened plant-based milk)

1 tablespoon fresh lemon juice

½ cup vegan butter, melted

sage cracker topping

2 cups crumbled saltine crackers

2 tablespoons olive oil

1 tablespoon nutritional yeast

2 teaspoons dried rubbed sage

½ teaspoon freshly cracked
black pepper

Sea salt

assembly

1½ cups vegetable broth

½ cup chopped celery,
including leaves

Fresh sage leaves, for garnish
(if desired)

5. Transfer the batter to the baking dish and bake for
30 minutes. At this point, once baked, you can let cool and
place in the fridge overnight until you are ready to serve or
skip to the next step.

6. When ready to serve, preheat the oven to 350°F.

7. **Make the sage cracker topping:** In a small bowl, mix together
the crumbled saltines, olive oil, nutritional yeast, sage,
pepper, and salt to taste.

8. **To assemble:** Using a fork, dishevel and stir the stuffing. Add
the vegetable broth for moistness, chopped celery for an extra
kick of freshness, and the sage cracker topping for crunch.
Coat the top with vegetable oil spray. Bake until thoroughly
hot and golden on top, about 30 minutes. Serve.

glazed carrots

SERVES 4 TO 6

These glazed carrots are the perfect companion to any meal and also great on their own. If you can pick up fresh carrots from the farmers' market to make them—even better. The sweet maple syrup, salty and tangy miso, and sharp whole-grain mustard give this dish an incredibly satisfying taste. Roasting the carrots brings out their gorgeous sweetness. Seriously finger-lickin' good.

1 pound rainbow carrots, peeled and halved lengthwise

4 large shallots, peeled, rinsed, and quartered

2 tablespoons olive oil

2 tablespoons maple syrup

2 tablespoons Creole or whole-grain mustard

2 tablespoons mellow white miso or chickpea miso

2 tablespoons nutritional yeast

2 teaspoons rice vinegar

2 teaspoons tamari

2 teaspoons sriracha (optional)

1. Preheat the oven to 350°F.

2. Throw the carrots, shallots, olive oil, maple syrup, mustard, miso, nutritional yeast, vinegar, tamari, and sriracha, if using, into a 9 × 13-inch baking dish and toss well, until all the carrots are coated.

3. Roast until the carrots are soft and tender, about 30 minutes, tossing halfway through. You can take them out earlier if you like a crunchier carrot.

turnip greens

SERVES 4 TO 6

I fondly remember eating turnip greens, although as a kid I honestly didn't know what a turnip was, never mind their green tops. I just did what I was told and ate my veggies! Now, whenever I spot a beautiful bunch of turnips at the farmers market I can't help but stock up on a few bunches. Every Southerner has their own way of making turnip greens. Some mix the turnip greens (they can be bitter) with other greens such as mustard, collards, or kale. I don't mind their bitterness, but I also like adding in another variety of greens just for fun, so I do. Some Southerners boil the greens in a large pot of water with a ham hock, bacon, or chicken stock. I use vegetable stock, liquid smoke, rice vinegar, and tamari to replace this pump of flavor. I find them to be just as good, if not better. So give it a go for yourself and let me know what you think!

6 cups shredded turnip greens (tops only, thoroughly washed)

6 cups shredded mustard, collard, or kale (lower stems removed, thoroughly washed)

1 cup vegetable broth

1 cup diced onion

1 tablespoon minced garlic

1 teaspoon rice vinegar

1 teaspoon maple syrup

2 teaspoons tamari

Splash liquid smoke

Sea salt and pepper, to taste

Place all of the ingredients except the salt and pepper into a large pot and mix well. Bring to medium-high heat, stirring often. Once bubbling, place the lid on top and cook for 5 minutes. Remove the lid and lower the heat to medium. Cook the greens, stirring frequently, until most of the liquid has evaporated and the greens are tender, succulent, and juicy, 10 to 15 minutes. Season with salt and pepper and serve.

lagniappe: *If you can't find turnip greens, you can use whatever hearty green you can find. For example, you could simply use just 12 cups of shredded kale if that's all you could find and you would have a fantastic dish on its own. No matter what the large leafy green, I don't bother de-stemming, as it's a personal preference in texture. I do remove the lower parts of stems, where there is little to no leaf, but aside from that, it all tastes good to me!*

green bean casserole

SERVES 8

I totally love me some green bean casserole. But it's been ages since I've had the classic recipe that so many Americans make for Thanksgiving. I call my Thanksgiving celebration "Thanksvegan," and over the years I've created my own rendition of a traditional green bean casserole. I'm pretty sure it's much cooler than the other kind. Like, way cooler. Instead of adding a can of cream of mushroom soup, which has God-knows-what in it and has been sitting on a shelf for God-knows-how-long, I figured out a way to make my own. For that concentrated mushroom flavor, I make my own base by blending dried shiitake mushroom into a powder and then adding raw cashews, water, and a handful of herbs and spices. The result is a thick mushroom cashew cream, which is a super delicious vegan variation of cream of mushroom soup! Ayy! Next, I blanch fresh green beans until they are bright green instead of using mooshy, lifeless canned green beans. After they bake, the beans are succulent with just a touch of crispness. As for the crispy onion topping, don't worry, store-bought versions are usually vegan and there are a few organic brands on the market.

---

2 tablespoons rice vinegar

Sea salt

1½ pounds green beans, trimmed and cut into bite-size pieces

1½ cups packed dried shiitake mushrooms

3 cups filtered water

1 cup raw cashews, soaked

2 tablespoons nutritional yeast

1 tablespoon tamari or coconut aminos

1 teaspoon onion powder

1 teaspoon garlic powder

Freshly cracked black pepper

6 ounces crispy onions, or to taste

1. Preheat the oven to 375°F.

2. Fill a large pot with water and add the vinegar and 1 tablespoon of sea salt. Bring to a boil and add the green beans. Cook for exactly 2 minutes. Drain the beans and transfer them to a 9 × 13-inch baking dish. Set aside.

3. In a blender, blend the dried mushrooms into a powder. Add the water, cashews, nutritional yeast, tamari, onion powder, garlic powder, tamari, and sea salt and black pepper to taste and blend until smooth, adding a bit more water if needed to help blend. Pour over the green beans and mix well. (Don't worry if it looks a little liquidy, the cashew cream thickens up quite a bit once baked.)

4. Bake for 45 minutes. Remove from the oven and sprinkle the crispy onions on top. Bake until golden brown on top, an additional 10 to 15 minutes. Serve.

kumquat broccolini

with toasted gomashio

SERVES 2 TO 4

Kumquats grow in the most southern parts of the South, where deep freezes don't happen often. My first memory of them was a small tree that my grandmother had on her patio. I was always fascinated by them: such beautiful bright orange clusters. Some people might enjoy eating them on their own, but they can also give a dish a ton of flavor, and this recipe is a perfect example. I've cooked the kumquats down with salty tamari, spicy ginger, and a splash of vinegar to make a mouthwatering sauce for broccolini. My Toasted Gomashio (page 268) adds the final touch.

1 pound Broccolini, rinsed

½ cup fresh orange juice

1 teaspoon grated lemon zest

2 tablespoons fresh lemon juice

½ teaspoon ume plum vinegar

3 tablespoons vegetable oil

3 tablespoons thinly sliced kumquats, seeded

2 garlic cloves, minced (or Microplaned)

2 tablespoons tamari

½ teaspoon fresh ginger, minced (or Microplaned)

2 tablespoons filtered water

1 tablespoon cornstarch

Sea salt

Toasted Gomashio (page 268), for serving

1. In a large skillet or pot, combine the Broccolini, orange juice, lemon zest, lemon juice, vinegar, vegetable oil, kumquats, garlic, ginger, and tamari. Mix well and bring the sauce to a simmer.

2. Meanwhile, in a small bowl, mix together the water and cornstarch until smooth. Pour into the sauce. Mix well and cook for another minute or two.

3. Once the sauce has thickened, and the Broccolini and cook until it is tender yet still crunchy, remove from the heat.

4. Transfer to a platter, sprinkle with the gomashio, and serve.

okra & tomatoes

SERVES 4 TO 6

One of my favorite vegetable sides has always been stewed okra and tomatoes. Growing older, I realized that I much prefer my vegetables not cooked to death. That's why I decided to try roasting this recipe in a high-heat oven instead of cooking it down until mushy, which is more traditional. Simply throw everything in a skillet and pop it in the oven. After roasting, the delicious juices from the ripe tomatoes and young, tender okra fall to the bottom of the pan and the hefty amount of green onions flavor the newly created sauce even more. Before serving, give the mixture a good toss until everything is coated. Absolutely delicious. And talk about easy.

1 pound young, tender okra, washed

1 pound ripe cherry tomatoes, rinsed

1 cup thinly sliced green onions, plus some for garnish

3 tablespoons vegetable oil

2 tablespoons nutritional yeast

1 teaspoon rice vinegar

1 teaspoon sea salt, plus more to taste

½ teaspoon freshly cracked black pepper, plus more to taste

1. Preheat the oven to 450°F.

2. Place all of the ingredients in a 9 × 13-inch baking dish and mix well. Once the oven is piping hot, place the mixture inside. Roast for 20 minutes. Remove and mix well. Garnish with more green onions and salt and pepper to taste.

lagniappe: *When it comes to green onions, I cut off the lower root and an inch or two off of the top (usually the dried-out part) and use the rest. I usually reserve the lighter green parts for garnish, as I find them to be the prettiest.*

mashed potatoes

with rosemary miso mushroom gravy

SERVES 4 TO 6

White, fluffy, buttery, and rich. How can mashed potatoes *not* be the definition of comfort food? If I'm feeling any pain or sorrow, with just one or two bites, those feelings simply melt away. So props to mashed potatoes for making the world just a *little* bit better. And it's hard to imagine a bowl of mashed potatoes being anything less than perfect on its own. Hard to imagine, that is, until you try this Rosemary Miso Mushroom Gravy.

---

3 pounds russet potatoes, peeled and cut into large chunks

1 tablespoon + 1 teaspoon sea salt

½ cup plain unsweetened plant-based milk, plus more if needed

½ cup vegan butter

Dash freshly grated nutmeg

Freshly cracked black pepper to taste

Rosemary Miso Mushroom Gravy (recipe follows)

1. Add the potatoes to a large pot. Sprinkle in 1 tablespoon of salt and cover with water. Bring to a boil and reduce the heat to a simmer. Cook until the chunks are fork-tender, about 30 minutes. Drain and return to the pot.

2. Add the milk, butter, nutmeg, black pepper to taste, and the remaining 1 teaspoon salt. Using a potato masher, mash the potatoes vigorously until light and fluffy. Add more milk to reach your desired creaminess. Serve immediately with the gravy.

> **lagniappe:** *To make super light and fluffy mashed potatoes, use a hand mixer and beat until desired texture is achieved. I quite like lumps of potatoes in my mash, as it implies they're homemade.*

rosemary miso mushroom gravy

SERVES 4 TO 6

½ cup peanut oil or light olive oil

½ cup all-purpose flour

2 cups chopped mushrooms (cremini/baby bella or shiitakes)

1 cup chopped onion

1 tablespoon nutritional yeast

2 tablespoons chopped garlic

1 tablespoon mellow white miso or chickpea miso

1 tablespoon chopped fresh rosemary or 2 teaspoons dried

5 cups vegetable broth

1 to 2 teaspoons tamari

Sea salt and freshly cracked black pepper, to taste

This gravy is bursting with flavor. Toasting the flour and nutritional yeast creates a deep, nutty taste, and the caramelized onions and garlic bring a sweetness. Sautéed mushrooms and miso provide a rich savoriness, while rosemary adds the perfect floral notes. Blend it together and you have a velvety, smooth gravy that you could honestly pour over anything and be happy. As you probably already guessed, this gravy should be included on every holiday table.

1. In a large skillet, stir the oil and flour over medium heat. Cook, stirring constantly, until the flour begins to lightly brown, about 5 minutes.

2. Add the mushrooms, onion, and nutritional yeast and cook, stirring frequently, until the onions and mushrooms are soft and golden brown, about 10 minutes. Add the garlic, miso, and rosemary. Mix well and cook for a few more minutes. Whisk in the vegetable broth and tamari and bring to a simmer.

3. Remove from the heat and transfer to a blender. Blend until smooth and serve hot. Or, if making ahead, store in the fridge. When ready to serve, reheat in a small pot over medium-low heat, adding water to achieve your desired consistency while mixing well. Season with salt and pepper to taste and serve hot.

roasted cauliflower

SERVES 4 TO 6

This is my go-to recipe for when guests come over. People simply can't get enough! The key is roasting the florets at a high temperature—the thick coating crisps up to a golden crust, while the inside stays tender and juicy. The best part? The small tidbits that get slightly burned at the bottom of the pan. You'll be scraping it up with your fingers. Promise.

¼ cup nutritional yeast

3 tablespoons vegetable oil

1 tablespoon tamari

1 tablespoon whole-grain or Dijon mustard

1 teaspoon grated lemon zest

1 tablespoon fresh lemon juice

1 teaspoon garlic powder

1 teaspoon onion powder

½ teaspoon freshly cracked black pepper

⅛ teaspoon cayenne pepper

5 cups golf ball–size cauliflower florets (1 head)

Sea salt

1. Preheat the oven to 450°F. Line a baking sheet with parchment paper.

2. In a large bowl, whisk together the nutritional yeast, vegetable oil, tamari, mustard, lemon zest, lemon juice, garlic powder, onion powder, black pepper, and cayenne pepper. Add the cauliflower and gently toss to coat each piece thoroughly. Season with salt to taste.

3. Arrange the cauliflower on the lined baking sheet and roast until crispy on the outside and fork-tender, about 30 minutes.

blood orange cranberry sauce

SERVES 4 TO 6

This sauce is the classic side dish for any holiday table. And guess what? It is traditionally 100 percent vegan! Can you believe it? There is actually a *fully vegan* recipe that makes its way to every Thanksgiving table in America, and we don't even think about it. Who'da thought? To make it just a bit fancier, I add a touch of fresh ginger and I use blood orange juice and zest, but you can surely use regular oranges. You just won't be as cool as me. But that's okay, babe.

One 12-ounce bag fresh cranberries

½ cup sugar

1 tablespoon grated blood orange zest

½ cup fresh blood orange juice, plus more if needed

1 teaspoon minced fresh ginger (optional)

Sea salt

1. In a small pot, combine the cranberries, sugar, orange zest, orange juice, ginger, if using, and salt to taste. Gently bring to a boil over medium-high heat, then reduce the heat to medium-low and cook, stirring occasionally, until the cranberries begin to pop. Cook until the sauce becomes thick, about 10 minutes. (Note that the sauce will thicken as it cools.) If desired, crush the cranberries using a fork or potato masher.

2. Remove from the heat and allow to cool. Serve immediately or store in the fridge until ready to serve. Feel free to add a splash of water or orange juice to loosen the sauce before serving.

sweet potato casserole

with vegan marshmallow topping

SERVES 8

I can't help but laugh when I think how it's totally acceptable to put marshmallows on top of a vegetable dish. Like, who even thought of that? Well, whoever did was actually kind of genius. There's something magical about that fluffy, sweet, and crispy crunch on top of creamy, piping-hot sweet potatoes. When I made this dish for my friend, she said, "Oh, you're good." I responded, "I can't take credit! It's totally a classic." But I did add a lovely depth of flavor with orange zest and juice. A touch of allspice and cayenne brings in just a slight pop of spiciness that makes things interesting. If you are wondering about how you'll find vegan marshmallows, don't you fret for one itty-bitty minute. They are available at your local health food store and are actually just as good as the real deal.

---

3 pounds sweet potatoes, peeled and cut into 1½-inch chunks

1 tablespoon rice vinegar

1 tablespoon + 1 teaspoon sea salt, or to taste

½ cup vegan butter

⅓ cup plain unsweetened plant-based milk

½ teaspoon grated orange zest

¼ cup fresh orange juice

½ cup packed light brown sugar

1 teaspoon ground cinnamon

1 teaspoon freshly grated nutmeg

¼ teaspoon ground allspice

¼ teaspoon cayenne pepper (optional)

Two 10-ounce bags vegan marshmallows

1. Preheat the oven to 350°F.

2. In a large pot, combine the sweet potatoes, vinegar, and 1 tablespoon of sea salt. Add filtered water to cover the potatoes by a few inches and bring to a boil. Cook until the potatoes are fork-tender, about 15 minutes. Drain in a colander and return to the pot. Throw in the vegan butter, milk, orange zest, orange juice, brown sugar, cinnamon, nutmeg, allspice, cayenne, if using, and the remaining 1 teaspoon salt. Using a hand mixer, beat until fluffy.

3. Transfer to a 9 × 13-inch baking dish and plop the marshmallows on top, covering the potatoes completely (you may not need to use all of the marshmallows, and that's okay). Bake until the tops of the marshmallows are beautifully browned, about 30 minutes.

roasted pumpkin

with cheesy walnut crumble

SERVES 6

Juicy and succulent, roasted pumpkin is a treat indeed. The combination of tangy miso and rice vinegar with a touch of nutmeg and cayenne pepper truly highlights its subtle flavor. A hefty sprinkling of a cheesy walnut crumble takes this dish from ordinary to extraordinary.

pumpkin

8 cups peeled pumpkin cut into 1½-inch cubes (about 3 pounds)

¼ cup vegetable oil

2 tablespoons coconut sugar or brown sugar

2 tablespoons mellow white miso or chickpea miso

1 tablespoon rice vinegar

½ teaspoon sea salt

¼ teaspoon freshly grated nutmeg

¼ teaspoon cayenne pepper

cheesy walnut crumble

½ cup walnuts

3 tablespoons nutritional yeast

½ teaspoon fresh lemon juice

¼ teaspoon sea salt

Fresh thyme sprigs, for garnish

1. Preheat the oven to 400°F. Line a baking sheet with parchment paper.

2. In a large bowl, toss the pumpkin cubes with the oil, coconut sugar, miso, vinegar, salt, nutmeg, and cayenne. Spread evenly on the baking sheet and bake until the chunks are tender and golden, about 40 minutes.

3. **While the pumpkin is roasting, make the walnut crumble:** Spread the walnuts into an even layer on a baking sheet or baking dish and roast in the oven along with the pumpkin for 8 minutes, or until slightly toasted and fragrant. Remove and add the nutritional yeast to the pan. Pop back in the oven for an additional 2 minutes to toast the yeast. Once done, remove and transfer the mixture to a food processor and add the lemon juice and sea salt. Pulse to create a crumble. Set aside.

4. Once the pumpkin chunks are done, transfer to a serving dish. Serve sprinkled with the walnut crumble and garnish with the fresh thyme sprigs.

roasted green meat radishes

SERVES 4

I love green meat radishes for their starchy, yet tender texture—think a potato that's tender and juicy. I grow these myself after seeing them popping up at farmers' markets. They're not only fun to grow, but the green tops are totally edible and delicious as well. When it comes to really good, fresh produce, I love to use simple flavors that enhance the vegetable, rather than compete with it. You can absolutely use traditional red radishes, although they are juicier than the green meats and come across as watery to some. If you've never tried roasted radishes, I think you will be pleasantly surprised.

2 bunches green meat radishes, tops removed

1 tablespoon olive oil

2 teaspoons rice vinegar

1 teaspoon sea salt, or to taste

½ teaspoon freshly cracked black pepper, or to taste

Dash cayenne pepper (optional)

2 to 3 tablespoons nutritional yeast

1. Preheat the oven to 450°F.

2. Cut the larger radishes into fourths and the smaller ones in half. Transfer to a large skillet or parchment-lined baking sheet. Toss with the olive oil, vinegar, salt, pepper, and cayenne, if using, until well combined. Sprinkle with nutritional yeast.

3. Roast until the radishes are crispy on the outside, about 45 minutes, tossing halfway. Serve immediately.

scalloped root casserole

SERVES 4 TO 6

Imagine this: thinly sliced potatoes, beets, and butternut squash arranged in beautiful layers and stuffed with a savory blend of garlic, fresh rosemary, olive oil, and dried herbs. Then baked until golden brown and tender. What else do you need to know?

1 large russet potato, peeled

1 medium golden beet, peeled

1 medium butternut squash neck (the top half of the squash), peeled

3 tablespoons olive oil, plus more if needed

3 tablespoons minced garlic

1 tablespoon fresh rosemary, plus sprigs for garnish

1 tablespoon nutritional yeast

1 teaspoon dried thyme

1 teaspoon dried oregano

1 teaspoon sea salt, or to taste

½ teaspoon freshly cracked black pepper, plus more for serving

1. Preheat the oven to 350°F.

2. Using a mandoline, cut the potatoes, beets, and butternut squash into thin rounds about ¼ inch thick. Once sliced, cut the rounds in half, creating half-moons. You will assemble the casserole by sandwiching layers of the vegetables into a small baking dish or loaf pan. Make three layers of potatoes, three of butternut squash, then three more potatoes, and then a layer of yellow beets. Repeat until the baking dish is stuffed. To give you an idea, you are basically creating an accordion of vegetable slices.

3. In a mortar (or a food processor), combine the olive oil, garlic, rosemary, nutritional yeast, thyme, oregano, salt, and black pepper. Mash or blend until you are left with a smooth paste.

4. Spread the paste over the sandwiched vegetable slices, pressing it gently down into the cracks, but not disrupting the design. Wrap tightly with foil and bake for 30 minutes. Remove from the oven and remove the foil. Increase the temperature to 400°F. Return to the oven and bake uncovered until the top is crispy and golden brown, an additional 20 to 30 minutes.

5. Serve garnished with rosemary sprigs and sprinkled with black pepper.

sesame-roasted brussels

SERVES 4

I love this recipe because it comes together quickly and it's incredibly scrumptious. The crunchy, peppery sprouts are an ideal vegetable for roasting at a high temperature because they crisp up nicely on the outside, while becoming tender and juicy in the center. The lemon juice provides a touch of brightness, while the sesame seeds are toasted to perfection during roasting, which pairs beautifully with a drizzle of toasted sesame oil. This is one of my favorite vegetable sides. It's a winner.

1 pound Brussels sprouts, cleaned, ends trimmed, and quartered

1 tablespoon olive oil or vegetable oil

1 tablespoon raw sesame seeds

1 tablespoon nutritional yeast

1 teaspoon rice vinegar

1 teaspoon fresh lemon juice

½ teaspoon sea salt, or to taste

½ teaspoon freshly cracked black pepper, or to taste

1 tablespoon toasted sesame oil, for serving

1. Preheat the oven to 500°F (or the highest your oven will go). Line a large baking sheet with parchment paper.

2. In a large bowl, toss the Brussels sprouts with the oil, sesame seeds, nutritional yeast, vinegar, lemon juice, salt, and pepper until well combined. Spread into an even layer on the baking sheet. Roast until the edges are crispy and slightly browned, 15 to 20 minutes. Drizzle on the sesame oil and toss. Serve immediately.

skillet okra

SERVES 2 TO 4

My first memory of okra was when I was four years old. I'm not kidding! I had a flashback memory of an old lady frying up some okra in a cast-iron skillet, telling me to "Get!" when I got in her way. When I asked my mother about this memory, she said, "Oh yeah, that was Mrs. LaCuesta! She was the neighborhood woman that mothers would drop their kids off to when we needed to run errands. You called her Maw Maw." Now, how on earth could I remember such a thing? Well, because she was frying okra, that's why. To this day, it is still one of my all-time favorite vegetables. Try adding a sprinkling of corn grits while cooking to give this dish a fun little crunch.

1 pound okra pods

2 to 3 tablespoons vegetable oil

1 tablespoon rice vinegar

1 tablespoon nutritional yeast (optional)

1 tablespoon corn grits (optional)

Sea salt and freshly cracked black pepper to taste

1. Rinse the okra thoroughly and pat dry with a paper towel. Remove any stems from the top, but leave the caps of the okra on.

2. Add the oil to a large cast-iron skillet and gently roll it around until it covers the bottom of the skillet. Set the skillet over high heat. Once the oil begins to smoke, throw in the okra and cook, stirring frequently, until browned on their sides, 2 to 3 minutes.

3. Throw in the vinegar, nutritional yeast, if using, corn grits, if using, salt, and pepper and cook for another minute or two. You want the okra to be golden brown on the outside but still have a nice crunch in the middle. Season with more salt if desired and serve immediately.

lagniappe: *Often people remove too much of the okra vegetable when they are prepping it. The tops and bottoms are both edible—you only have to trim off the fibrous stalks that connect to the caps. Also, when you are shopping for okra, look for the young, small pods as they are the most tender and delicious.*

—

CHAPTER 7

desserts

highly sophisticated chocolate chip cookies

with rosemary & pecans & other fun things

MAKES 12 COOKIES

I expect a lot out of a chocolate chip cookie. Not only does it have to be vegan, I'm also looking for a handful of characteristics. Crispy and crunchy while also chewy. Salty yet not too sweet. The perfect amount of chocolate and butteriness. All the while with a depth of flavor. That's precisely why this recipe was created. Now, it may not be for everyone. And that's okay. There are loads of plain, basic chocolate chip cookie recipes out there. This isn't one of them. Fresh rosemary, black pepper, and nutmeg amuse the tongue; while coconut sugar, molasses, and flaxseeds provide the perfect chew. Toasted pecans and oat flour provide a subtle nuttiness. A sprinkling of flaked Maldon salt pushes these cookies over the top, in the best way possible. All in all, these are my go-to chocolate chip cookies. They're a bit more on the savory side and, well, highly sophisticated.

---

1 cup coconut sugar

¾ cup vegan butter, softened

2 tablespoons finely chopped fresh rosemary

¼ teaspoon freshly cracked black pepper

¼ teaspoon freshly grated nutmeg (or ground)

¼ cup plain unsweetened plant-based milk

1 tablespoon ground flaxseed meal

½ teaspoon sorghum molasses

2 teaspoons vanilla extract

½ teaspoon almond extract

1 cup all-purpose flour

⅓ cup oat flour

½ teaspoon baking soda

¼ teaspoon sea salt

1. Preheat the oven to 350°F. Line two large baking sheets with parchment paper.

2. In a large bowl, combine the coconut sugar, butter, rosemary, black pepper, and nutmeg. Beat with a fork until smooth and fluffy. Add the milk and flaxseed meal and beat for another 30 seconds. Mix in the molasses, vanilla, and almond extract. Set aside.

3. In a separate bowl, combine the flours, baking soda, and salt. Mix well. In small amounts, slowly add this mixture to the wet mixture, mixing constantly until it forms a dough. Fold in the pecans. Refrigerate the dough for 30 minutes to chill.

4. Using an ice cream scoop or spoon, scoop about 2 tablespoons of dough for each cookie onto the baking sheets, leaving a few inches between them. They will spread out as they bake.

recipe and ingredients continue

recipe continued from previous page

½ cup roughly chopped toasted pecans

3 ounces vegan dark chocolate, roughly chopped

1 to 2 teaspoons Maldon salt, for sprinkling

1 to 2 teaspoons vanilla sugar (see page 36), for sprinkling

5. Arrange the chocolate chunks on top of each mound of dough and press them down gently. Sprinkle with the Maldon salt and vanilla sugar. Bake until the edges are golden brown, but not burned, 15 to 20 minutes. Let cool on the baking sheets for about 5 minutes, then transfer them to a cooling rack for another 5 minutes.

bananas foster

SERVES 4 TO 6

This recipe originated at the famous New Orleans–based restaurant Brennan's. Since its creation, it's become a popular dessert at many restaurants throughout the South. Traditionally, bananas Foster is made to order, right at the table. As a young boy, I remember watching our server effortlessly flambé this decadent combination of bananas, butter, sugar, and a splash of rum. Theatrics aside, this dessert is actually quite easy and you can make it in your very own home. It literally comes together in *minutes*. Serve over your favorite vegan ice cream and watch it melt into oblivion. This is also the perfect topping for the Toasted Pecan Waffles (page 46). Before you get started, be warned that the sugar can burn. Make sure to keep the sauce moving, watch the heat, and keep the cooking process as short and sweet as possible. Practice makes perfect!

½ cup vegan butter

1 cup coconut sugar

½ teaspoon ground cinnamon

4 bananas, peeled, halved lengthwise, and cut into 2- to 3-inch pieces

¼ cup dark rum

1 tablespoon vanilla extract

Vegan vanilla ice cream, for serving (optional)

1. In a heavy-bottomed sauté pan, melt the butter over medium-high heat. Stir in the coconut sugar and cinnamon. Whisk until the sugar dissolves and the sauce is bubbling.

2. Add the bananas and sauté until softened, stirring occasionally. Remove the pan from the heat. Add the rum and vanilla extract, then carefully return the pan to the heat. Once the rum begins to release vapor, very carefully use a BBQ lighter to light the alcohol on fire, standing back from the flames. When the flames subside, stir the mixture, remove from the heat, and serve over vanilla ice cream, if desired.

lagniappe: *If you have never flambéed (set alcohol on fire while cooking), I suggest you hop online to watch someone do it. There are loads of tutorials. If you still don't feel comfortable doing this, simply add less rum and don't worry about setting it on fire. It will still taste just fine.*

strawberry shortcake crunch bars

with coconut whipped cream & pecan shortcake crust

MAKES ABOUT 12 BARS

Do you remember those strawberry shortcake ice cream bars that you had as a kid? The kind with the crunchy outside? Well, this is my vegan-ized version in a handheld bar form. You're welcome. The shortcake crust has turbinado sugar, which provides a delightful crunch, while the pecans help out with the butteriness (they can't help it—that's just what they do). And what could be a better vehicle for shoveling whipped coconut cream studded with juicy strawberries into your mouth? I grew up going strawberry picking as a young boy with my parents, and once we arrived home, we would douse our freshly harvested berries with heavy whipping cream and a healthy sprinkling of sugar and gobble it up. There's really nothing better than that. Well, except these bars.

shortcake crust

1 cup unrefined coconut oil, refrigerated until hardened

½ cup turbinado sugar

⅛ teaspoon sea salt

2 cups all-purpose flour

½ cup chopped pecans

coconut whipped cream

Two 13.5-ounce cans full-fat coconut milk, refrigerated overnight

1 teaspoon vanilla extract

Pinch sea salt

½ cup powdered sugar

1 pint strawberries, cut into ¼-inch-thick slices

1. Preheat the oven to 350°F. Line a 9 × 13-inch baking dish with parchment paper.

2. **Make the shortcake crust:** In a bowl, using a fork or hand mixer, cream together the coconut oil, turbinado sugar, and sea salt until fluffy. Slowly mix in the flour until everything is incorporated. Fold in the chopped pecans.

3. Evenly spread the batter into the baking dish. Bake until the edges are slightly golden brown, 35 to 40 minutes. Set aside to cool completely.

4. **Make the coconut whipped cream:** Remove the tops from the coconut milk cans and scrape the firm coconut cream into the bowl of a stand mixer or a large bowl. (Discard the liquid or set it aside for another recipe.) Fit the mixer with the whisk attachment or use a hand mixer and blend the cold cream until smooth. Add the vanilla and salt. Mix well. Slowly sift in the powdered sugar, while beating, in increments. Scrape down the sides and continue to whip until light and fluffy, about 5 minutes.

recipe continues

recipe continued from previous page

lagniappe: *You can read more about coconut cream on page 37. Try studding these bars with other fresh berries such as blackberries, blueberries, or raspberries. The coconut whipped cream is truly the perfect glue to hold any variety of toppings.*

5. Using a large spoon or spatula, spread the whipped cream evenly over the cooled crust. Press in the strawberry slices in a beautiful arrangement. Refrigerate for at least 1 hour. Slice the bars into desired shapes and serve immediately. Note that the whipped cream melts quickly!

double buttery crust

If you've never made homemade pie crust, this is a good place to start. It's from my friends Isa Chandra Moscowitz and Terry Hope Romero's book *Vegan Pie in the Sky*. It's a classic go-to that works every time! If you are in a pinch, don't beat yourself up if you have to pick up a perfectly good premade vegan crust from the health food store. Traditional grocery stores even carry accidental vegan pie crust as well. Just make sure to check the ingredients.

2½ cups all-purpose flour

½ teaspoon sea salt

3 tablespoons sugar

½ cup cold vegan butter, cut into ½-tablespoon chunks

½ cup cold vegan shortening

4 tablespoons ice water

1 tablespoon apple cider vinegar

1. In a large bowl, sift together the flour and salt. Mix in the sugar. Add half the butter and shortening, cutting them into the flour with your fingers or a pastry blender, until the flour appears pebbly. Cut in the remaining butter and shortening.

2. In a measuring cup, mix together the water and vinegar. Drizzle the mixture into the flour by the tablespoonful, gently mixing it after each addition. Knead the dough a few times, adding more water until it holds together. You may need only the 4 tablespoons, but add up to 2 more tablespoons if needed.

3. Divide the dough in two, roll each half into a ball, then press them into disks and wrap each in plastic wrap. Refrigerate them until ready to use, or use as directed in the recipe.

apple rose tart

SERVES 8

Here's a fancy spin on the classic apple pie. Of course, I would never pass up a homemade-looking pie, imperfections and all. But this variation is just too pretty to not try at least once. And I bet after you make it, you'll make it again and again! Be forewarned: This is a *weekend* dessert that takes *a lot* of time. This is the kind of dessert you bring to your significant other's parents *the first time you meet them.* Get my drift? This is the kind of dessert that will leave people talking, you feel me? As it turns out, this is the kind of dessert that is just as delicious as it is gorgeous, which, as most of you know, isn't always the case.

½ batch Double Buttery Crust (page 235) or one 9-inch store-bought vegan pie crust

½ cup roughly chopped toasted walnuts

1¼ pounds Granny Smith apples

1¼ pounds pink-fleshed apples

1 large lemon, halved

⅓ cup vegan butter, melted, plus more for brushing

½ cup vanilla sugar (see page 36)

½ cup packed light brown sugar

1 teaspoon ground cinnamon

½ teaspoon freshly grated nutmeg

¼ teaspoon ground allspice

¼ teaspoon ground cloves

¼ teaspoon sea salt

1. Preheat the oven to 425°F.

2. Fit the pie dough into a regular pie dish. Poke holes in the dough with a fork and place a piece of parchment on top. Fill the pie shell with dried beans to prevent bubbles. Bake for 15 to 20 minutes. Remove the beans, sprinkle in the toasted walnuts, and set aside. Leave the oven on.

3. Using a mandoline, slice the apples into ⅛-inch-thick rounds. Then slice the rounds in half. Transfer the slices to a bowl and squeeze the lemon juice on top to prevent browning.

4. Pour steaming-hot water over the apples. Let them soak for a few minutes, until they are soft enough to manipulate. Drain off the water and leave the apples in the bowl.

5. In a small bowl, whisk together the melted butter, vanilla sugar, brown sugar, cinnamon, nutmeg, allspice, cloves, and sea salt. Pour the mixture over the sliced apples and gently toss.

6. Delicately roll the slices into rose shapes, placing them into the pie crust as you go. Once tightly filled, transfer to the oven and bake until the apples are tender and the kitchen smells like apple pie, 25 to 35 minutes. Brush with melted butter and serve.

hummingbird cake

with cream cheese lemon glaze

MAKES 1 LOAF

The first time I had hummingbird cake was at a birthday party in Athens, Georgia. After one bite, I was hooked. With the combination of ripe bananas and pineapple and a hint of cinnamon and toasted pecans, sweet Jesus, it's perfection. It's no wonder this is a classic Southern dessert. Traditionally, this recipe is served as a three-layer cake with cream cheese frosting. But I decided to streamline this recipe, making it much more efficient and less labor intensive. Instead of using multiple cake pans, simply pour the batter into a traditional loaf pan. The glaze is super easy to make and tastes delicious drizzled over the cake. Garnish with edible flowers, thinly sliced pineapple, or a sprinkling of toasted pecans. Whatever you'd like!

cupcakes

1½ cups all-purpose flour

¾ cup vanilla sugar (see page 36) or regular sugar

½ teaspoon baking soda

½ teaspoon ground cinnamon

½ teaspoon sea salt

¾ cup vegetable oil

½ cup unsweetened applesauce

1 cup mashed ripe bananas (about 2 large)

½ cup canned crushed pineapple, undrained

1 teaspoon vanilla extract

½ cup chopped pecans

cream cheese lemon glaze

2 ounces vegan cream cheese

2 teaspoons grated lemon zest

1 teaspoon fresh lemon juice, plus more as needed

1¼ cups sifted powdered sugar

1. **Make the cake:** Preheat the oven to 350°F. Grease and lightly flour a 9 × 5-inch loaf pan.

2. In a large bowl, sift together the flour, sugar, baking soda, cinnamon, and salt. In a separate bowl, combine the vegetable oil, applesauce, mashed banana, crushed pineapple, and vanilla. Mix until smooth. Pour the applesauce mixture into the bowl with the flour mixture and mix with a fork, scraping down the sides as needed, until everything is incorporated. Fold in the pecans. (Please do not overmix.) Transfer to the prepared loaf pan.

3. Bake in the center of the oven for 50 minutes to 1 hour, until a toothpick comes out clean and the cake is springy to touch. Cool in the loaf pan for 10 minutes. Remove from the pan and cool on a wire rack for 30 minutes before glazing.

4. **While the cake cools, prepare the cream cheese glaze:** Mix together the cream cheese, lemon zest, and lemon juice. Slowly sift in the powdered sugar, mixing constantly. Depending on desired thickness, add more lemon juice to loosen. Using a large spoon, drizzle desired amount of glaze over the cake and serve.

peach cream pops

MAKES 12 POPS

My favorite ice cream flavor is peach. But guess what? I've never seen vegan peach ice cream. Like, *ever*. Is that some kind of sick joke? Well, instead of pouting, I decided to take matters into my own hands by creating this recipe. I love to use popsicle molds to make these ice cream pops, but you can throw this recipe in a loaf pan to make ice cream, too. Just let it soften up a bit before scooping. Personally, I think popsicles are more fun. They're cute, they're handheld, and there's something that's so very nostalgic about them, wouldn't you say?

Three 13.5-ounce cans full-fat coconut milk

2 tablespoons unrefined coconut oil

1 tablespoon vanilla extract

1½ cups powdered sugar

1 teaspoon cornstarch

Dash salt

1 cup small chunks peeled peaches

1. Place the cans of coconut milk into the fridge overnight or for at least 6 hours.

2. Remove the tops of the cans and scrape out the firm coconut cream into a large bowl. You need 2 cups. (Discard the liquid or set it aside for another recipe.) Add the coconut oil and vanilla and, using a hand mixer, blend until smooth. Slowly sift in the powdered sugar, cornstarch, and salt while blending. Whip on high speed until the mixture becomes light and fluffy. Fold in the peaches.

3. Disperse the mixture evenly into a 12-cavity popsicle mold, leaving a little room at the top so they do not overflow while freezing. Place the popsicle mold lid on top and press in popsicle sticks, leaving about 1 inch or so out. Place the mold in the freezer and leave overnight.

4. To serve, run hot water quickly on the outside mold of whichever popsicle you would like to remove. Using a firm grip, pull the popsicle out and serve.

∫ lagniappe: *Read more about coconut cream on page 37.*

mama's pralines

MAKES 20 TO 30 PRALINES

More like candy than dessert, my mama has been making pralines ever since I can remember. When I was home visiting, I explained to her that she could easily vegan-ize them by replacing the dairy butter with vegan butter and using coconut cream instead of heavy cream. The next morning, she opened the door to my room with a twinkle in her eye and quietly said, "It worked." Sure enough, a beautiful batch of vegan pralines was downstairs waiting for me. They were just as I remembered, but maybe a little bit better. To make sure this recipe works perfectly, I highly recommend investing in a candy thermometer to be exact.

One 13.5-ounce can full-fat coconut milk, refrigerated overnight

2 cups coconut sugar

1 cup sugar

⅛ teaspoon sea salt

4 cups pecan halves, toasted

1 teaspoon vanilla extract

1. Line two large baking sheets with parchment paper.

2. Open the can of refrigerated coconut milk and scrape out the hard cream into a large saucepan, discarding the liquid. Add the sugar and sea salt to the cream. Cook over medium-high heat, stirring until smooth, until the ingredients are melted, about 5 minutes.

3. When you see the mixture beginning to bubble slightly, reduce the heat to medium-low. Place the candy thermometer in the pot. Bring the mixture up gradually to 238°F while only stirring occasionally. This should take about 8 minutes. Do not go higher than this temperature or the pralines will become hard like rock candy!

4. Remove the pot from the heat and stir the mixture. Stir in the pecans and vanilla to combine.

5. Using a large spoon (or a 2-tablespoon scoop), scoop heaping tablespoons of the mixture onto the lined baking sheets. The goal is to create a small pool of caramel with 4 to 5 pecans per cluster. Let them sit at room temperature for about 45 minutes, or until completely frosted in color.

6. Enjoy immediately or store between layers of parchment paper in a container at room temperature. These also freeze beautifully!

mini peach cobblers

with toasted almonds

MAKES 4 TO 6 MINI COBBLERS

Lucky for me, my friends up at Cherry Creek Orchards in Pontotoc, Mississippi, grow some of the best peaches this side of the Mississippi! And when it comes to peaches, my mind goes straight to peach cobbler. It has to be one of my favorite desserts. Juicy, sweet peaches baked under a flaky crust? C'mon, you know you want some. I've made this recipe even better by adding chopped almonds to the crust, which provides a nice crunch. A splash of almond extract deepens that flavor in a beautiful way. I've also made the executive decision to make them mini so there's more crust and everyone gets enough. You'll thank me later. If you don't have access to good, ripe peaches, that's okay. You can use frozen. But I can't tell you how much better this dessert is when you use fresh, ripe ones.

4 cups chopped juicy ripe peaches (6 medium)

¼ cup vanilla sugar (see page 36) or regular sugar, plus more for sprinkling

2 tablespoons unrefined coconut oil

½ teaspoon grated lemon zest

1 tablespoon fresh lemon juice

2 teaspoons vanilla extract

½ teaspoon almond extract

1 tablespoon cornstarch

1 teaspoon ground cinnamon

½ teaspoon sea salt

½ batch Double Buttery Crust (see page 235) or one 9-inch store-bought vegan pie crust

¼ cup chopped blanched almonds

Vegan vanilla ice cream, for serving (optional)

1. Preheat the oven to 350°F.

2. In a large pot, combine the peaches, sugar, coconut oil, lemon zest, lemon juice, vanilla, almond extract, cornstarch, cinnamon, and sea salt. Cook over medium-high heat until the mixture begins to bubble. Cook until the mixture reduces to a glossy, thick consistency, about 5 minutes. Distribute the mixture among 8- to 12-ounce ramekins.

3. Cut the dough into thin strips (¼ inch thick) and weave on top of each filled ramekin. Brush or spray the crusts with vegetable oil. Sprinkle almonds and sugar on top.

4. Place the ramekins on a baking sheet. This will make it easier to transfer in and out of the oven. Bake until the crust is golden brown, about 40 minutes.

5. Serve as is or with your favorite vegan vanilla ice cream.

lagniappe: *I like to leave the peach peel on. If the texture bothers you, simply peel the peaches before cutting them. For a more rustic look, simply cut the crust into circles and place them over each ramekin. Cut some slits on top to let the steam out when baking.*

pecan tassies

MAKES 8 MINI PIES

There is an abundance of pecan trees growing all over the South, especially in Mississippi. Heck, there are three trees in my backyard! As you can guess, you can't avoid using this buttery, sweet nut in Southern cuisine. One great way to use them is to make pecan tassies. This recipe is roughly based on the traditional recipe and veganized, of course. I prefer to use coconut sugar and brown rice syrup, as I find them to be more flavorful than white sugar. A splash of bourbon pairs beautifully with the caramelly flavor.

Double Buttery Crust (page 235) or two 9-inch store-bought vegan pie crusts

¼ cup brown rice syrup

¼ cup coconut sugar

1 tablespoon melted vegan butter

½ teaspoon vanilla extract

Splash bourbon (optional)

Dash sea salt

2 tablespoons filtered water

1 teaspoon cornstarch

2½ cups chopped pecans

1. Preheat the oven to 350°F.

2. **Prepare the crust:** Roll the pie dough out until it is approximately ¼ inch thick. Using a small circular cookie cutter, cut small rounds of dough just less than 3 inches in diameter to form the piecrust for two 12-well mini pie shell pans or muffin pans (you will be making a total of 24 mini pies). Set aside.

3. **Make the filling:** In a large bowl, whisk together the brown rice syrup, coconut sugar, melted butter, vanilla, bourbon, if using, and salt. In a separate small bowl, whisk together the water and cornstarch until the mixture becomes a smooth paste. Add the cornstarch mixture to the sugar mixture and mix well. Fold in the pecans until thoroughly incorporated.

4. Distribute the filling evenly among the mini pie shells, leaving some room at the top. Keep in mind that if the filling bubbles over too much, it will make it very difficult to remove the mini pies from the pan. Less is more.

5. Bake the pies in the middle of the oven for 25 minutes, or until the crust is golden brown. Let cool for 20 minutes and serve.

lagniappe: *I place my pans on a larger baking sheet to make them easier to place and remove from the oven. You may need to use a butter knife to help the mini pies pop out of the pan.*

CHAPTER 8

—

sauces,
condiments
& staples

creole spice blend

This spice blend was created for seasoning all of my gumbo recipes. Traditionally, gumbo recipes call for many animal-based ingredients, including smoked meats, ham hock, bacon, or butter. Obviously all these ingredients are flavorful on their own. And because none of these are used in my gumbo, I've compensated for their lack of flavor by upping the spice content. Classic dried herbs in combination with ground sage, cumin, and smoked paprika help to create a vegan gumbo spice blend that is incredibly flavorful.

½ cup nutritional yeast

1 tablespoon onion powder

1 tablespoon garlic powder

1 teaspoon dried oregano

1 teaspoon dried parsley

1 teaspoon dried thyme

1 teaspoon smoked paprika

1 teaspoon smoked or plain
  sea salt

½ teaspoon cayenne pepper

½ teaspoon dried ground sage

½ teaspoon ground cumin

½ teaspoon ground white pepper

½ teaspoon freshly cracked
  black pepper

Mix all of the ingredients together in a small bowl until well combined. Keep in a tightly sealed jar until ready to use.

mushroom
rice paper bacon

SERVES 6

I first stumbled upon the idea of rice paper bacon when my mama heard about it. That night I made my first batch. The idea is you toss strips of rice paper with seasonings and bake them until crispy, somewhat like bacon. I thought that first batch was good, but it wasn't great. There was something missing. Then I had the brilliant idea to sandwich thin slices of mushrooms in between the crispy layers of rice paper to provide a chewy texture and savory flavor. Guess what? It worked. For even more flavor, I add a glaze of mustard, maple syrup, and tamari on the outside. The result is mushroom rice paper bacon.

⅔ cup peanut oil

¼ cup nutritional yeast, plus more for sprinkling

3 tablespoons tamari or coconut aminos

1 teaspon liquid smoke, plus more to taste

24 shiitake mushroom caps, thinly sliced (about 6 cups packed)

1 pack (6-inch) rice paper wrappers

glaze

1 tablespoon whole-grain mustard

1 tablespoon maple syrup

1 tablespoon tamari

2 tablespoons oil

1. Preheat the oven to 350°F. Line two large baking sheets with parchment paper.

2. In a large bowl, whisk together the peanut oil, nutritional yeast, tamari, and liquid smoke. Throw in the mushrooms and mix well.

3. To assemble, wet your cutting board to help prevent the rice paper from sticking. Wet one sheet of the rice paper with some water (in a bowl of water or under the faucet) and place it on the cutting board. Massage the rice paper gently for a few seconds. Spread on a thin layer of the marinating mushrooms in a 1-inch-thick line down the middle of the wet wrapper. Fold the sides over the mushrooms, creating a rectangular strip, and carefully transfer to baking sheet. Repeat this step until all the mushrooms are gone.

4. Whisk together the glaze ingredients and brush over the top of the bacon strips. Sprinkle some nutritional yeast on top and bake for 30 minutes. Remove and flip them with a spatula. Bake for an additional 15 minutes, or until crispy and golden brown. Let cool for 10 minutes and enjoy.

the art of making shiitake bacon

SERVES 4 TO 6

The reason I call this the "art" of making shiitake bacon is because that is precisely what it is. There is an art form to creating the perfect batch. I can only attempt to show you how, the best way that I can. The rest is up to you. Please remember, every oven is different. Cooking times will vary. The ultimate goal? To bake the mushroom slices until they are crispy and chewy at the *very same time*, replicating that distinct bacony texture we all know and love. Good luck!

1 pound stemmed shiitake mushroom caps (about 2 pounds before trimming)

¾ cup peanut oil

½ cup tamari or soy sauce

½ cup + ½ teaspoon nutritional yeast, plus some for dusting

1 teaspoon liquid smoke, plus more to taste

1. Position racks in the center and bottom third of the oven and preheat the oven to 375°F. Line two large baking sheets with parchment paper.

2. Rinse the shiitake caps and dry them thoroughly in a salad spinner or pat them dry with a paper towel. Cut the caps into ¼-inch-thick slices (the goal here is to have similar-size pieces so that they cook evenly). Transfer them to a large bowl.

3. In a small bowl, whisk together the peanut oil, tamari, ½ cup of the nutritional yeast, and the liquid smoke. Pour this mixture over the sliced shiitakes. Delicately toss them until all the pieces are coated. Divide the mushrooms evenly onto the baking sheets, arranging them into a single layer.

4. Sprinkle the remaining ½ teaspoon nutritional yeast on top of the shiitakes and coat the tops with a healthy amount of cooking oil spray. (The goal here is to basically oven-fry the shiitakes, so please don't hold back—this isn't a low-fat recipe. We are replicating bacon, people.)

5. Place the sheets in the oven, one in the center, one on the bottom. Bake for 40 minutes. Remove from the oven and toss with a thin spatula. Spread the mushrooms back out evenly and coat them again with a good amount of cooking oil spray, and another dusting of nutritional yeast. Return the trays to the oven, switching racks. Bake until the mushrooms become crispy on the edges, about 15 minutes (less if you think they might burn). Remove from the oven.

6. At this point you could make or break the bacon. And because each oven is different, you have to play with it yourself. What you are trying to do is push the mushrooms to their crispiest point without burning them. As my mother would say, you must "Watch them like a hawk!" Coat the mushrooms once more with some cooking oil spray and return to the oven for an additional 5 to 10 minutes. Remove from the oven and let sit for a few minutes. Taste one. If it is still not crispy, bake for an additional 5 to 10 minutes. If you are scared to keep pushing it, try only baking a few to see how far you can take them. This way you won't burn the whole batch.

7. One baking sheet may be done before the other; just remove them at separate times. Some pieces may also be stubborn and take longer than others. It's okay if a few pieces are chewier than others. Like the recipe implies, making shiitake bacon is an art. It takes practice to perfect this exquisite food.

lagniappe: *Depending on which brand of liquid smoke that you are using, you may be able to add more, which will give your bacon a smokier flavor. Just be careful, as some brands are stronger and more bitter than others. After adding 1 teaspoon, give the mixture a taste. If you'd like to splash some more in, feel free to do so!*

sunshine kimchi

SERVES 8

This vibrant kimchi is crunchy, zesty, and tangy—the perfect addition to salads, sandwiches, and wraps or thrown into fried rice or a vegetable stir-fry. As for traditional kimchi, it includes garlic, ginger, and napa cabbage. To spin it my own way, I add fresh turmeric root, which provides the cabbage with a beautiful yellow glow. I like my kimchi to have a kick, so I throw in some chili peppers, but you can totally leave that out if you'd prefer. When purchasing the Napa cabbage head, make sure to weigh one that is over 2½ pounds, as you will be removing the green parts. The goal is to be left with 2 pounds for the batch of kimchi.

---

1 large head Napa cabbage (a little over 2½ pounds)

½ cup filtered water

¼ cup chopped onion

5 garlic cloves, peeled

1½ tablespoons freshly chopped fresh turmeric

1½ tablespoons freshly chopped fresh ginger

3 teaspoons sea salt

½ teaspoon cayenne pepper (optional)

lagniappe: *Make sure to leave at least 2 inches of room at the top of the jar so that the kimchi does not overflow while fermenting. If you do cram the kimchi into a smaller jar, just remember that it is going to expand and bubble, and likely overflow all over the counter (it's happened to me a few times!). If you are using a smaller jar, place it in a bowl just to be safe.*

1. Remove the outer leaves of the cabbage head. Chop off the darker green leaves on top (to keep the bright yellow color of the finished kimchi). Cut the cabbage into 2-inch squares so that you are left with exactly 2 pounds and transfer to a large bowl.

2. In a blender, combine the water, onion, garlic, turmeric, ginger, sea salt, and cayenne, if using, and blend into a smooth paste. Pour this mixture over the cabbage.

3. Using your hands, deeply massage the cabbage, bruising the pieces and making them soft and pliable.

4. Transfer the mixture to a large screw-top jar (I recommend a 1-gallon-size jar; see lagniappe) and press the mixture down so that it is mostly submerged in liquid. Tap the bottom of jar to get rid of any air bubbles.

5. Screw on the top of the jar (not too tight) and leave it out to sit in a dark, cool place for 5 days. Remember to burp the jar, opening the lid to release accumulated gases, once or twice a day for the first few days. After 5 days, try a small piece. You'll know it's done when it tastes tangy and delightfully sour and has a nice crunch. Refrigerate overnight and start enjoying the next day! Keep tightly sealed in the fridge for up to 1 month.

blueberry bbq sauce

SERVES 6 TO 8

Barbecue sauce is no doubt a popular condiment throughout the United States, but it is particularly beloved in the South. And there is plenty of controversy over who makes the best. I honestly don't care because I'm too busy eating my unique variation. Blueberries are my secret ingredient and they make a tangy, sweet sauce with a gorgeous purple hue. Lucky for you, this sauce comes together very quickly and easily with pantry staples—the only ingredients you most likely will have to purchase are good blueberry preserves and a pint of fresh blueberries. Bonus points for picking your own blueberries and buying a jar of preserves from an old lady named Mammy on the side of the road.

One 12-ounce jar blueberry preserves

1 teaspoon onion powder

1 teaspoon garlic powder

1½ cups filtered water

One 6-ounce container blueberries

One 6-ounce can tomato paste

¼ cup packed brown sugar, or to taste

1 tablespoon rice vinegar

1 tablespoon tamari

2 teaspoons vegan Worcestershire sauce

2 teaspoons liquid smoke

1 teaspoon sea salt

½ teaspoon chili powder

½ teaspoon Microplaned fresh ginger

¼ teaspoon cayenne pepper

1. In a medium saucepan, mix together the blueberry preserves, onion powder, and garlic powder to form a paste. Add the water, blueberries, tomato paste, brown sugar, vinegar, tamari, Worcestershire sauce, liquid smoke, sea salt, chili powder, ginger, and cayenne and mix well. Bring the mixture to a boil over medium heat, stirring often.

2. Reduce the heat to low and simmer for 20 minutes. Remove from the heat. Use immediately or leave to cool and transfer to a tightly sealed jar and keep in the fridge for up to 1 week.

rémoulade

MAKES 1½ CUPS

This traditional French condiment is usually served with breaded seafood, like crab cakes (or better yet, my Happy Crab Cake Bites on page 91). Recipes vary greatly across the board, but the common denominator is mayo, fresh herbs, and pickles or capers. My version has red wine vinegar for a subtle tanginess and horseradish for a kick. You can easily play with this recipe, removing and adding whatever you'd like.

1 cup vegan mayo

2 tablespoons finely chopped fresh parsley

1 tablespoon minced celery

2 teaspoons minced shallots

2 teaspoons capers, chopped

2 teaspoons prepared horseradish

2 teaspoons whole-grain mustard

2 teaspoons red wine vinegar

2 teaspoons fresh lemon juice

1¼ teaspoons sweet paprika

1 teaspoon sugar

½ teaspoon minced garlic

½ teaspoon onion powder

½ teaspoon nutritional yeast

Sea salt and freshly cracked black pepper

In a bowl, stir together the mayo, parsley, celery, shallots, capers, horseradish, mustard, vinegar, lemon juice, paprika, sugar, garlic, onion powder, nutritional yeast, salt, and pepper to taste. Keep in a tightly sealed jar in the fridge for up to 3 days.

homemade mayo

MAKES ABOUT 1½ CUPS

Don't get me wrong, I know store-bought mayo is a breeze. But did you know that you can make your very own at home as well? Traditionally, mayo recipes use egg yolks, which have sulfur. To make up for this flavor, I use kala namak as the salt, which has naturally occurring sulfur. I know this may sound overpowering, but it's not. It's actually quite subtle and provides a nice depth of flavor. You can easily double this recipe if you need to.

½ teaspoon kala namak salt

1 teaspoon sugar

1 teaspoon dry mustard

2 teaspoons rice vinegar

1 teaspoon lemon juice

½ cup cold, plain unsweetened almond milk

1½ cups sunflower oil

1. Place the kala namak, sugar, dry mustard, rice vinegar, lemon juice, and milk in a high-speed blender. Blend for 15 seconds on high speed. Reduce the speed to medium and add 1 cup of oil, a few tablespoons at a time, slowly. Increase the speed to high to blend until the mixture becomes thick and creamy.

2. Decrease the speed to medium and blend in the remaining ½ cup oil. The mixture might get stuck, as it will become thick. Try switching back and forth between low speed and high speed to get it moving. If you need to, turn off the blender and mix the top into the bottom with a utensil. Continue to blend until all the oil is mixed in thoroughly.

3. Using a spatula, transfer the mayo into a tightly sealed jar, place in the fridge, and chill until the mixture is firm. This will keep for a few days.

lagniappe: *If the blender is going for too long, it will create heat, which will then break the mayo, turning it into a useless oily mess. Fortunately, this mayo does come together quickly but just keep that in mind if you give this one a go.*

zesty ranch

MAKES ABOUT 4 CUPS

This isn't your simple salad dressing. It's much more complex, and it definitely is a bit more sophisticated than the traditional ranch you can buy at the store. It's loaded with fresh herbs and their dried counterparts, providing maximum flavor. Give it a go and take your salad greens to the next level. It's also a great dip for crudités, roasted potatoes, or Fried Pickles (page 87). Heck, you could eat this with anything.

½ cup chopped fresh dill

½ cup chopped fresh parsley

½ cup chopped fresh chives

1½ cups vegan mayo

¾ cup plain unsweetened plant-based milk

¼ cup fresh lemon juice

2 tablespoons apple cider vinegar

3 tablespoons nutritional yeast

2 garlic cloves, chopped

1 tablespoon mellow white miso or chickpea miso

1 tablespoon dried dillweed

1 tablespoon dried chives

1 tablespoon dried parsley

1½ teaspoons salt, or to taste

1 teaspoon freshly cracked black pepper

1 teaspoon sugar

1 teaspoon onion powder

1 teaspoon garlic powder

1. In a bowl, combine the fresh dill, parsley, and chives. Set aside.

2. In a blender, combine the mayo, milk, lemon juice, vinegar, nutritional yeast, garlic, miso, dried dill, dried chives, dried parsley, salt, pepper, sugar, onion powder, and garlic powder and blend until smooth.

3. Pour the mixture over the fresh herbs and mix well. Transfer to a tightly sealed jar and keep in the fridge for up to 1 week.

lagniappe: *By leaving the fresh herbs chopped and unblended, you are left with the m ore traditional speckled look of ranch. If you blend everything up together, you get a pastel green dressing, which might interest you!*

comeback sauce

MAKES ONE 16-OUNCE JAR

Comeback sauce is a dipping condiment that originated in Jackson, Mississippi, decades ago. There are many different variations of this delicious, creamy sauce, but this is my version. You can dip almost anything in this sauce, especially Fried Pickles (page 87).

1½ cups vegan mayo

¼ cup tomato-based chili sauce (see lagniappe)

¼ cup ketchup

1 tablespoon stone-ground or Dijon mustard

1 tablespoon sriracha (optional)

2 tablespoons minced onion

1 tablespoon minced garlic

1 tablespoon fresh lemon juice

1 teaspoon vegan Worcestershire sauce

1 teaspoon freshly cracked black pepper

Dash cayenne pepper

1. In a small bowl, stir together the mayo, chili sauce, ketchup, mustard, sriracha, if using, onion, garlic, lemon juice, Worcestershire sauce, black pepper, and cayenne.

2. Transfer to a tightly sealed container and keep in the fridge for up to 1 week.

lagniappe: *There are many different forms of chili sauce out there. The one I'm referring to has similar ingredients to traditional ketchup, and they are stocked closely together at the store.*

slow-roasted tomato jam

MAKES ABOUT 1 CUP

This jam is simple and elegant. Slightly sweet and tangy, with an underlying hint of cinnamon and cloves, this condiment is perfect for spreading on a hot biscuit or piece of cornbread.

1 quart cherry tomatoes

¼ cup olive oil for blending, plus 2 tablespoons for roasting

Sea salt

6 tablespoons sugar

2 tablespoons fresh orange juice

1 tablespoon fresh lemon juice

¼ teaspoon ground cinnamon

⅛ teaspoon ground cloves

Freshly cracked black pepper

1. Preheat the oven to 325°F. Line a baking sheet with parchment paper.

2. Add the tomatoes plus the 2 tablespoons of olive oil and 1 teaspoon of sea salt to the baking sheet and toss well. Pop them in the oven and bake until they are soft, squooshy, and caramelized, about 1 hour, stirring halfway through.

3. Transfer the mixture to a food processor and add ¼ cup of the olive oil, the sugar, orange juice, lemon juice, cinnamon, and cloves. Blend until smooth and jam-like in texture. Give it a taste and season with salt and pepper as needed. Transfer to a tightly sealed jar and enjoy. This should keep in the fridge for 1 to 2 weeks.

tabasco vinegar

MAKES 2 CUPS

This is a fun way to infuse plain vinegar with a kick of spice. Try adding just a splash on any rice dish, roasted or steamed vegetables, or in salad dressing to liven things up. Your taste buds will thank you.

1 cup Tabasco peppers, green tops removed

2 cups distilled white vinegar

1. Place the peppers in an 8-ounce glass jar.

2. In a small pot, bring the vinegar to a boil. Using a funnel, carefully pour the vinegar into the jar over the peppers and let sit until completely cool. Place the lid on top and let marinate for a few days before using.

homemade hot sauce

MAKES ABOUT 3 CUPS

This hot sauce is thick and has a gorgeous tangerine color. It's easy to execute, fresh, and, of course, spicy. Feel free to substitute any variety of hot peppers that you desire. Just make sure to wash your hands and cutting board thoroughly once done!

¼ cup vegetable oil

4 cups chopped onion

3 cups cayenne peppers, tops removed

⅓ cup chopped garlic

1 cup filtered water

½ cup distilled white vinegar

2 teaspoons sugar

1 tablespoon sea salt, plus more to taste

1. In a large skillet, heat the oil over medium heat. Add the onion, peppers, and garlic and sauté, stirring often, until soft, about 5 minutes. Remove from the heat and let cool.

2. Transfer the sautéed mixture to a food processor or high-powered blender and combine with the water, vinegar, and sugar. Blend until smooth. Add the sea salt to taste. Pour into a small jar. Keep tightly sealed in the fridge for up to 1 month.

toasted gomashio

MAKES ¼ CUP

Gomashio is a traditional Japanese condiment made of toasted sesame seeds muddled with sea salt. To make this classic condiment even more vegan than it already is, I like to add toasted nutritional yeast to the mix. This adds a nutty cheesiness that I'm sure you'll adore. Sprinkle it on salads, rice, or veggies.

¼ cup raw unhulled sesame seeds

1 teaspoon nutritional yeast

⅛ teaspoon sea salt

In a small pan or skillet, combine the sesame seeds, nutritional yeast, and sea salt. Dry-toast the mixture over medium-low heat, stirring constantly, until the mixture is fragrant and slightly golden, about 5 minutes. Transfer to a mortar and pestle and grind a good portion of the mixture until most of the sesame seeds are crushed, but some are still whole. If you don't have a mortar and pestle, transfer the mixture to a small bowl and use the back end of a kitchen utensil to crush the seeds. Serve immediately or keep stored in a tightly sealed jar for a few days. Immediately is best.

lauren's cashew parm

SERVES 4

When my friend Lauren Toyota of *Hot for Food* came down to visit me, she made this recipe. I walked into the kitchen and she had whipped up a batch in the blink of an eye. I said, "Excuse me, Miss Thing, what is that?" She rolled her eyes and smugly said, "Cashew Parm," as she sprinkled a hefty amount on a salad and walked out of the room. It's so easy and delicious, I knew I had to share it with all of you.

⅔ cup raw cashews or blanched almonds

¼ cup nutritional yeast

1 teaspoon sea salt

In a food processor, combine the cashews, nutritional yeast, and salt and process until a fine crumb or meal is formed. Store in a tightly sealed container in the fridge for up to 3 weeks. But it won't last that long.

vegan crack

MAKES ABOUT 1 CUP

This is vegan crack. I don't know what else to say. Once you try it, you'll understand. You don't have to be vegan to understand, either. Try sprinkling this magic dust on roasted vegetables, pasta, soups, salads—*anything, really.*

1 cup nutritional yeast

¼ cup olive oil

½ teaspoon dried oregano

½ teaspoon dried thyme

1 teaspoon crushed red pepper flakes (optional)

½ teaspoon sea salt, or to taste

½ teaspoon freshly cracked black pepper, or to taste

1. Preheat the oven to 350°F. Line a large baking sheet with parchment paper.

2. Combine the nutritional yeast, olive oil, oregano, thyme, pepper flakes, if using, sea salt, and black pepper on the lined baking sheet. Mix well with your fingers and spread into an even layer. Pop in the oven and bake until everything looks toasty and golden brown, 10 to 15 minutes, tossing once halfway through.

3. Remove from the oven and let cool. Pick up the sheet of parchment paper and fold up the sides to create a funnel shape. Transfer the crack to a bowl to serve immediately. Sprinkle on anything or eat alone with a spoon in a dark corner where no one is looking.

lagniappe: *I recommend keeping this in a tightly sealed jar in the fridge. Although, it honestly shouldn't last too long.*

CHAPTER 9

—

wellness

mushroom maca iced latte

SERVES 2

This is my go-to healthy pick-me-up on days when I'm busy in the kitchen or simply on my feet all day. I particularly love the way this latte sneaks in medicinal mushrooms. Feel free to play with any variety of them in this recipe: reishi, lion's mane, chaga, cordyceps, whatever you're feeling. I'm particularly drawn to reishi and lion's mane because they both grow wild here in Mississippi. I'm not kidding! On an afternoon jog, I'll see some reishi popping out of a tree, happy as can be! Flip on over to page 98 to see my harvest of wild lion's mane as well. But please: Don't feel as though you have to forage your own! There are many great companies that offer high-quality medicinal mushrooms dried and preground for your everyday use. Do your research to learn which mushrooms may benefit you the most.

To help mask the mushroom flavor, I use a good amount of leftover coffee (just make extra in the morning). It pairs beautifully with the maca powder, a Peruvian root known for providing stamina, and also provides a necessary punch of caffeine when you need it. The water and flesh of a young Thai coconut is truly unparalleled to any flavor—the buttery, rich water is packed with electrolytes and the flesh is full of good fats. Blended together, they make a smooth coconut cream that's completely raw and healthy. I throw in one to two Brazil nuts for selenium and a touch of blackstrap molasses for minerals. The dates provide an all-natural sweetener, while the nutmeg provides just a hint of spice. Absolutely delicious!

---

1 young Thai coconut

2 cups brewed coffee, cooled

2 to 3 pitted dates, for desired sweetness

2 raw Brazil nuts

2 teaspoons powdered reishi, lion's mane, cordyceps, or chaga

1 teaspoon unrefined blackstrap molasses

1 teaspoon maca powder

½ teaspoon freshly grated nutmeg

1. To open the coconut, use the bottom corner of a large chef knife or cleaver to strike the top of the coconut about 1½ inches from the pointed tip. Cut all the way around to form a hexagon shape and pry off the top gently. Pour the liquid into a high-powered blender.

2. To harvest the meat, use a large rounded spoon to scrape out the inside flesh of the coconut and add to the blender.

3. Add the coffee, dates, Brazil nuts, mushroom powder, molasses, maca powder, and nutmeg to the blender and let it go until smooth and creamy. Pour into large ice-filled glasses. Drink up with a straw.

lagniappe: *If you need help opening the coconut, go online—there are many video tutorials that can show you the best technique.*

bouillon tea

This tea is a cross between really good homemade broth and hot herbal tea. Instead of boiling a whole bunch of vegetables, I thought to myself, "Why not just juice them and add hot water?" This process intensifies the flavor of the vegetables and their nutrition. Just add water to easily puree and then squeeze the mixture through a cheesecloth. You'll be left with an excellent, potent, nutrient-dense bouillon broth concentrate. When ready to serve, pour some into a mug and top it off with hot water, lemon juice, and a pinch of sea salt. That's what I call bouillon tea.

2½ cups chopped celery

1 cup chopped fresh ginger

½ cup chopped fresh turmeric

½ cup chopped carrots

2 to 3 sprigs fresh parsley

1 teaspoon cayenne pepper

2 cups filtered water

Fresh lemon juice

Pinch sea salt (optional)

1. To make the tea concentrate, in a blender, combine the celery, ginger, turmeric, carrots, parsley, cayenne, and water and blend until smooth. Pour through cheesecloth draped into a fine-mesh sieve (set over a bowl). Pull the sides of the cheesecloth up around the pulp and squeeze out all of the juice. Transfer this concentrate to a mason jar and keep tightly sealed and refrigerated until ready to serve. (This will keep in the fridge for up to 3 days.)

2. When ready to serve, add some concentrate to a mug and pour in boiling water. My concentrate to water ratio is usually 1:4, but feel free to play with this. Squeeze over some lemon juice and, if desired, add a pinch of sea salt. Enjoy.

home-brewed herbal teas

There's nothing quite like snuggling up with a hot cup of tea, is there? Especially when they are homemade using beautiful ingredients. These are three of my favorite brews. Each ingredient provides a unique flavor profile while offering different nutritional benefits. Feel free to push and pull the steeping time to your liking. All three are delicious served hot or cold.

6 cups filtered water

4 fresh bay leaves or 4 young echinacea flowers, or 5 cinnamon sticks

1. In a small pot, bring the water to boil. Add the tea base of choice and boil for 1 minute. Remove from the heat, cover, and steep for about 15 minutes.

2. Remove the tea base and serve hot, or chill in the fridge and pour over ice when ready.

BAY LEAVES provide a slightly floral aroma reminiscent of thyme with a subtle spice. Once steeped, the water becomes a lovely soft pink color. Bay leaves are known to help aid in digestion and are packed with vitamins and minerals.

—

ECHINACEA is sought after for its immune-boosting qualities and overall promotion of skin health. I find their young flowers to have a mild licorice undertone that's quite pleasant in flavor while also creating a stunning tea presentation.

—

CINNAMON provides a potent tea base that tastes surprisingly sweet without the sugar. It's a fantastic source of manganese and has anti-inflammatory properties. I find the slight spice and familiar aroma to be incredibly comforting.

floral beard oil

MAKES 1 SMALL JAR

Making your own beard oil (whether it be for you or for someone you know with a beard) is a cost-effective and delightful way to ensure a happy, well-conditioned beard that also smells divine. The powerful combination of ylang-ylang and jasmine creates a scent that is absolutely intoxicating. It is best to apply beard oil directly after showering, when the hair follicles are soft and more receptive to absorption from the heat. Add a few drops of beard oil to your palms and rub them together, spreading the oil evenly around your palms and fingers. Massage the oil into your beard, using your fingertips to massage your hair in circular motions. Comb your beard gently with a brush. Finish by rubbing your beard downward with your palms, shaping your beard and pressing in any loose hairs. Apply once or twice a day.

One 1-ounce jar

Argan oil

20 drops ylang-ylang essential oil

20 drops jasmine essential oil

Fill the jar 85 percent with argan oil. Add the ylang-ylang and jasmine oils. Top the bottle off with more argan oil to fill it completely and tightly seal. This will keep for a few months.

calming face mist

MAKES ONE 12-OUNCE BOTTLE

I always have a bottle of this homemade face mist hanging around. Whenever I'm feeling stressed or overwhelmed, I simply spritz a mist or two of this on my face. Instantly, I feel just a little bit calmer. There's something incredibly calming about lavender and eucalyptus, in particular when they are transformed into a gentle mist.

One 12-ounce spray bottle

Filtered or spring water

40 drops eucalyptus essential oil

40 drops lavender essential oil

1. Fill the bottle to the top with water, leaving about ¼ inch of space. Add the essential oils. Screw the top on tightly.

2. For application, adjust the spray bottle to the mist setting. Before misting each time, shake the bottle thoroughly to mix. Spray 2 to 3 times about 10 inches away from the face as often as desired.

lagniappe: *You can easily scale down this formula to fit whatever size bottle you have available. You can store the bottle in the fridge to make this mist even more refreshing.*

acknowledgments

Dad, you gave me my green thumb, showed me roses, and taught me what it means to be kind. Thank you.

Mama, you always told me to shine my light. This is me shining as brightly as I can. Thank you for being my rock.

Aunt Mary, thank you for allowing me to harvest and photograph citrus from the best soil in Louisiana!

Aunt Jeannie and Laura, thank you for the Meyer lemons, kumquats, and for bringing me to Bergeron Pecans.

To my local Mississippi Farms: Taylor Yowell at The Garden Farmacy, Two Dogs Farm, Foot Print Farms, Amorphous Gardens, Bountiful Harvest Farms, Cherry Creek Orchards, Salad Days Produce, and A Little Time to Grow. Thank you for providing me with gorgeous local produce.

Cara Janelle, thank you for providing me with your stunning ceramic work, much of which is on most of these pages. And thank you for visiting me all the way from Barcelona to help me with this book. You're my chica!

Isa, thank you for the countless FaceTime laughs, therapy sessions, and for being the funniest person in my life. I love you.

Diana, thank you for the endless hours of phone conversations, taking the most beautiful photographs of me, and sharing your delicious food.

Megan Elizabeth, thank you for coming all the way from Hawaii to visit and help me. I want you to know that you inspire me to be the healthiest version of myself that I can be, which is invaluable.

To my interns, Daniel, Alex, Nick, Sarah, and Barrett—look at what y'all helped me do! Thank you.

Patricia—to this day, I still think of you as an angel that was sent to me from the universe. I can't thank you enough for the tremendous amount of help you've provided. You will always be my vegan star.

Dave McGill, thank you for the all the plants.

Katie B—my baby. You helped keep me stay sane after moving all the way from New York City to Mississippi. You and Hugo will forever have my heart!

Lauren, since coming to visit me and helping me with this book, you've become one of my best friends. I couldn't have asked for more.

Pamela Elizabeth, you will always be on my speed dial.

Hillary and Justin, thank you both for coming to babysit me with this project! The work you both helped me with is on many of these pages. Thank you for all the laughs.

Monique, thank you for opening up your home and allowing me to make a huge mess in your kitchen. Our hard work paid off! I'm so thankful to have your support. To more great memories.

Alex Palmour, thank you for scrolling through thousands of images to help me choose the very best for this book. You've been a supportive friend of mine since I was sixteen. I love you.

Nate Burrows, thank you for lending me your eyes. Your feedback and support was absolutely crucial for this book.

Megan Clapton, you befriended me when I was new to Jackson, no questions asked. You then introduced me to some of the beautiful content that will forever be printed in this book. Thank you.

To my recipe testers, Amy Wierer, Kimberley Dockery, Gordon Blasco, Claire Jacobs, Anita Albright, Desiree Derr, Rachel Lake, John Boller, Erin Kay Hearns, Jessika Griffin, Aet Piiskoppel, Erin Pineda, Chloe Colwill, Deb Sobel, David Scott, Lisa Dawn Angerame, Lindsay Gruis, Karen Burns Botvinick, Tammy de Nobrega, Brooke Ritchie, Marie Lambert, Lila Taff, Cara Leonard, and Allison Chang. Boy, did you guys help me out! The recipes in this book would not be as effective without you.

Bella, your endless support, inspiration, and brainstorming has been invaluable toward the process of writing this book. I love you.

Meg and Cindy, since the day I met both of you, my life has forever changed. Thank you.

Amy Chaplin, thank you for your support and showing me what it looks like to put all of your heart into a cookbook.

Donna Hay, thank you for paving the way for food stylists everywhere and for inspiring elegance.

Linda Lomelino, thank you for showing me that food photography can be touching and emotional.

Mary Louise and Leda Meredith, thank you for teaching me about wild foods and foraging.

Jamie Oliver, your support has meant the world to me throughout my journey. Thank you for believing in me.

To my team at Avery—Lucia, thank you for believing in me and helping me sharpen my vision. Ashley, you had to put up with one picky author! You did a fantastic job. Thank you.

To my followers and fans, whether it be through my images, my stories, or my recipes—you've been there for me. You are my friends. This book would be nothing without you.

And to the state of Mississippi. Thank you for the soil, the oak trees, the mushrooms, the butterflies, the sunsets, and for being my home.

index

Page numbers in *italics* refer to photos.

—

TIMOTHY PAKRON is a passionate cook, recipe developer,
photographer, and creator of the blog *Mississippi Vegan*.
Before devoting himself to the culinary arts, he spent
time as a fine artist and freelance photographer in
Charleston, South Carolina, and New York City.
He currently lives and works in New Orleans.

—